Late Anti

Marcus Aurelius offering incense at the start of a sacrifice. Behind the emperor an old man stands for the Senate. In the background is the Temple of Jupiter Capitoline, god of state (Rome, Museum of the Conservators.)

Late Antiquity

Peter Brown

The Belknap Press of
Harvard University Press
Cambridge, Massachusetts
and London, England

Originally published as "Antiquité tardive" in Histoire de la vie Privée,
vol. I, *De l'Empire romain à l'an mil,* © Editions du Seuil, 1985, translated by Arthur
Goldhammer as *A History of Private Life*, vol. I: *From Pagan Rome to Byzantium*,
Harvard University Press, 1987.

Library of Congress Cataloging in Publication Data

Brown, Peter Robert Lamont.
   [Antiquité tardive. English]
   Late antiquity / Peter Brown.
      p.   cm.
   "Originally published as 'L'antiquité tardive' in Histoire de la vie
privée, vol. 1, De l'Empire romain à l'an mil, Editions du Seuil,
© 1985"—T.p. verso.
   Includes bibliographical references and index.
   ISBN 0-674-51170-0 (pbk.)
    1. Rome—Civilization.   2. Byzantine Empire—Civilization—527–1081.
    3. Rome—Social life and customs.
I. Title.
DG7413   1998
937—DC21   97-42973

Contents

✋ Introduction

I N four centuries, between the reigns of Marcus Aurelius
(161–180) and Justinian (527–565), the Mediterranean
world passed through a series of profound transmutations that
affected the rhythms of life, the moral sensibilities, and the
concomitant sense of the self of the inhabitants of its cities,
and of the countryside around them. During the late antique
period there was a slow shift from one form of public community to another—from the ancient city to the Christian
church. The life of the individual, the life of the family, even
matters as intimate as the perception of the body itself came
to be seen in relation to changing social contexts, associated
with the rise of new forms of community.

Tomb, 2nd–3rd century. Although the man buried here lived in remote if urbane Germania, he nevertheless found a sculptor of the right school to execute his tomb. The master wears a magnificent costume and holds a scroll; the lady is slender, and the child knows what pose to strike. The foliage is rich, and the folds of the robes are rendered in a highly decorative manner. (Trier, Landesmuseum.)

✍ The "Wellborn" Few

IN order to measure the nature and extent of the transformation that began with the "civic" man of the age of the Antonines and ended with the good Christian member of the Catholic Church of the Western Middle Ages, the theme must be allowed to wander, like a winding river, throughout the length and breadth of Roman Mediterranean society. It washes past many banks, touching on issues as intimate and as "private" (in the modern sense) as the changing meaning of marriage, of sexuality, of nudity. Yet during these centuries the river was fed by a concern largely alien to modern persons. Whether it be in the life of the notables of an Antonine city or in the habits of a late Roman Christian, we meet at every turn an ancient sense of need for a public community—for a community in which the experiences of the private individual were permeated at every level by the values of the community and were frequently expected, in ideal conditions, to be totally transparent to these public values. The way men and women in specific social contexts in the Roman world guided their lives in the light of changing notions of the public community to which they sensed they belonged provides insight into the history of the private life of Western Europeans.

Certain features of the Mediterranean world remained surprisingly constant throughout late antiquity. Topographically, we will seldom leave the cities. Each city was a little world of its own, defined by an intense awareness of its own status vis-à-vis that of its neighbors. "Daddy," asked a little boy in a third-century joke book, "do other cities have a moon as big as ours?" Status demanded an enduring and intimate connection with the city. In our joke book, a rich landowner altered the numbers on the milestones on the road leading to his country villa, in order to lessen the distance between his

Page from a manuscript of Virgil, 4th or 5th century. The illustration is not all appropriate to the text it accompanies, and the manuscript is a failed work of art. (Rome, Vatican Library.)

Villa of Piazza Armerina, first half of 4th century. The undressed woman wears a brassiere and artfully shields her lover from a frontal view. And for good reason, because the lover is probably Priapus, identifiable from the fruits carried in the fold of his raised garment and from the woman's wig that he often wore.

properties and *his* city! For all classes the anonymity of a modern city was almost totally absent. A woman whose husband had been crucified was advised by the rabbis to leave town—unless the city were as big as Antioch. The norm against which the elites measured their actions was the face-to-face society of the city.

In every city a crushing sense of social distance between the notables, the "wellborn," and their inferiors was the basic fact of Roman Imperial society. The most marked evolution of the Roman period was the discreet mobilization of culture and of moral grooming to assert such distance. The upper classes sought to distinguish themselves from their inferiors by a style of culture and moral life whose most resonant message was that it could not be shared. They created a morality of social distance that was closely linked to the traditional culture of the cities. At the very center of this culture and its attendant morality was the need to obey the rules for interchange between upper-class citizens in conducting the public business of the city.

Education gave the child to the city, not to the school. Physically, the *pedagogus* began by leading the seven-year-old boy from his house to the forum, where his teachers sat, in ineffectively screened-off classrooms abutting on this main center of urban life. Here he would be absorbed into the peer group of young men of similar status. He would owe as much to that peer group as to his teacher. The contents of this education and the manner and the place in which it was communicated aimed to produce a man versed in the *officia vitae*—in those solemn, traditional skills of human relations that were expected to absorb the life of the upper-class male.

A literary education was considered part of a more intimate and exacting process of moral grooming. It was firmly believed that the meticulous internalization of the literary classics went hand in hand with a process of moral formation: correct forms of verbal interchange manifested the upper-class citizen's ability to enter into the correct form of interpersonal relations among his peers in the city. A studied control of deportment, quite as much as of language, was the mark of the wellborn man on the public stage. Behavior which today we might dismiss as irrelevant—the careful control of gestures, of eye movements, even of breathing—was scrutinized for signs of successful conformity to the moral norms of the upper classes. The unbroken succession of laudatory epithets lavished on notables in the gravestones of Asia Minor from the Hellenistic age to the reign of Justinian betrays more than wishful thinking. The central role of adjectives stressing controlled and harmonious relations with peers and city, to the almost total exclusion of all other values, betrays the oceanic weight of expectations that pressed upon the successful male.

What could almost be called "moral hypochondria" formed a firm barrier between the elites and their inferiors. The harmonious person, groomed by long education and shaped by the constant pressure of his peers, was thought to live at risk. He was exposed to the ever-present threat of "moral contagion" from anomalous emotions and actions, inappropriate to his own public status though acceptable in the uncultivated society of his inferiors. I use "hypochondria" advisedly, for this was the age of great doctors—most notably, the doctor Galen (A.D. 129–199)—whose works circulated widely among the wellborn.

A specific body image, formed from a conglomeration

Social Distance

Mosaic of Susa, 2nd–4th century. Virgil seated on throne, holding a copy of the *Aeneid*, flanked by two Muses. The only image of a writer ever found on a mosaic features the greatest writer of all. Was this because the owner genuinely liked Virgil's poetry, or because, for all his reverence for culture, he did not go so far as to judge for himself the ranking of authors in the classical hierarchy?

Bronze tokens, showing various sexual positions on one side and numerals on the other. They must have been used in some sort of game.

of notions inherited from the long past of Greek medicine and moral philosophy, was the physiological anchor of the moral codes of the wellborn. In this model personal health and public deportment converged with the utmost ease. In it the body is represented as a delicately maintained balance of complementary humors, whose health was upset by excessive losses of needful resources or by excessive coagulations of detrimental surpluses. The emotions that were held to disrupt or deplete the carefully balanced deportment of the well-groomed man could be traced in large part to the effects of such imbalances. The body, therefore, was regarded as the most sensitive and visible gauge of correct deportment; and the harmonious control of the body, through traditional Greek methods of exercise, diet, and bathing, was the most intimate guarantor of the maintenance of correct deportment.

The status-based, inward-looking quality of a morality rooted in an upper-class need to demonstrate social distance by means of an exceptional code of deportment is immediately apparent in the moral concerns of the Antonine age. Relations with social inferiors and sexual relations, for example, are regulated in terms of an exacting code of public deportment. To beat a slave in a fit of rage was condemned. This was not because of any very acute sense that an act of inhumanity against a fellow human being had been committed, but because the outburst represented a collapse of the harmonious image of the self of the wellborn man, and had caused him to behave in a manner as uncontrolled as a slave.

Similar concerns determined attitudes toward sexual relations. Homosexual and heterosexual love were not distinguished. What was perceived as an underlying continuity between the two was the fact of physical pleasure. Sexual pleasure as such posed no problem to the upper-class moralist. What was judged, and judged harshly, was the effect of such pleasure on the public deportment and social relations of the male. Any shame that might be attached to a homosexual relationship resided solely in the moral contagion that might cause a man of the upper class to submit himself, either physically (by adopting a passive position in lovemaking) or morally, to an inferior of either sex. The relations of men and women were subject to the same strictures. Inversions of true hierarchy through oral sexuality with a female partner were the most condemned and, not surprisingly, the most titillating, forms of collapse before the moral contagion of an inferior, the woman. Fear of effeminacy and of emotional dependence, fears based on a need to maintain a public image as an effective upper-class male, rather than any qualms about sexuality itself, determined the moral codes according to which most notables conducted their sexual life.

The fear of social subservience to an inferior was subtly buttressed by physiological anxiety. A man was a man because he moved effectively in the public world. He did this because his fetus had "cooked" more thoroughly than had a woman's in the hot womb; his body, therefore, was a reservoir of the precious "heats" on which male energy depended. Although the difference between men and women might be securely fixed, in the case of the woman by the low ceiling of her heat and the consequent frailty of her temperament, there was no such security for the active man. His heat could be lost. Excessive sexual discharge might "cool" his temperament; such a drain on his resources would be betrayed with merciless precision in a loss of momentum on the public stage. That orotund voice of the public man that Quintilian and his con-

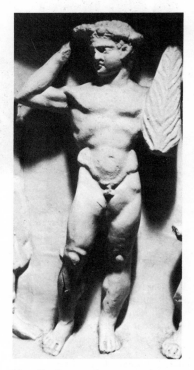

Detail of sarcophagus, 2nd century. This was either imported from Greece or done in imitation of Greek work. After winning a gymnastic contest, the ephebe dons the wreath that is the prize of victory and is awarded the palm by the man in charge of the games. (Rome, Vatican Museums.)

Marble marquetry, after 331. A solemn parade crosses Rome, headed for the Circus. Riding in the ceremonial chariot is the consul who will preside over and pay for the races, followed by the four chariot drivers who will compete. So many chariots are shown in profile in ancient art that it is interesting to see one head on. The frontal view results in a perspective that has been called "the exploded chariot"; even the wheels are splayed apart like the pages of a book.

temporaries so dearly loved to hear echoing through the noisy public spaces of the city was the fine fruit of a masculinity carefully preserved by "abstinence from sex." The very real puritanism of the traditional moralities of the upper classes of the Greek and Roman worlds rested heavily on those who subscribed to them. Such puritanism did not rest on sexuality; it rested on sexuality as a possible source of moral contagion. For sexual indulgence could erode, through the effeminacy that could result from excessive sexual pleasure with partners of either sex, the unchallenged superiority of the wellborn.

Hence the unquestioning particularity of the sexual codes of the age. They did not apply to everyone. The notables might tend to subject themselves and their families to a code of dour masculine puritanism, closer to that still current in Islamic countries than to the puritanism of modern northern Europe. Yet, having drawn the carapace of deportment around themselves, they found themselves all the more free to exhibit the other side of their public selves: their *popularitas*. In their relations, as givers of the good things of urban life, to their inferiors, they lavished on those assumed to have cruder pleasures than themselves a succession of displays, amenities, and paintings that flatly contradicted, in their cruelty and frank obscenity, the orderly self-control these men had arrogated to themselves as the badge of their own superior status in the city. Highly cultivated aristocrats patronized the appalling bloodshed of the gladiatorial games in the Greek cities of the Antonine age. Nor did the rise of Christianity greatly change this aspect of their public life. If a modern reader remembers anything about the emperor Justinian, it is likely to be Procopius' portrait of the youthful career of his wife, Theodora: a striptease dancer in the public theater of Constantinople, geese used to peck grain from her private parts in front of an audience of thousands of citizens. What is important to bear in mind is the venomous precision of this sketch. Here was a woman of the people, to whom upper-class codes of moral restraint did not apply. Theodora is the exact inversion of the respectable upper-class wives (soberly shrouded and even secluded in Constantinople, by that time). Yet, as notables, the husbands of such respectable ladies had for centuries donated just such performances, to the everlasting glory of themselves and of their city.

Nor is there anything surprising in the long survival of indifference to nudity in Roman public life. This was not a society bound together by the implicit democracy of sexual shame. Athletic nudity remained a mark of status for the wellborn. The essential role of the public baths as the joining point of civic life ensured that nudity among one's peers and

Mosaic of gladiators, dead and alive, with their names, 4th century. The patron who paid for the combat wished to preserve the names of the stars who fought and died at great expense to himself. Never were gladiatorial combats more deadly than in the 4th century, when sadism and munificence were at their peak. (Rome, Villa Borghese.)

in front of one's inferiors was a daily experience. The codes of deportment, as we have seen, reached down into the body itself; as a result, the clothes of the upper classes of the Antonine age, though expensive, lacked the ceremonial magnificence of later ages. How a man carried himself, in the nude or otherwise, was the true mark of his status—a mark all the more convincing because understated. As for women, the social shame of exposure to the wrong person, rather than the fact of exposure itself, was the principal anxiety. Nudity before one's slaves was as morally insignificant as nudity before animals; and the physical exposure of the women of the lower classes was yet another token of their disorderly inferiority to the powerful.

Empire and Order

In the cities of the Antonine age the facts of power weighed with all the unperceived mass of an atmosphere on the upper-class subjects of a world empire. However intimate the life of the average city might be, Rome was an empire, one founded on and protected by violence. The cruelty of the gladiatorial games was put on display as part of the official celebration of the Emperor in every great city of the Mediterranean. Such displays made plain the bloodthirsty will to rule of the Italian elite. Even the games played by the humble, as they tossed dice on the edges of the forum, were games of war. The moves designated on the counters were: The Parthians are killed; the Britons are conquered; the Romans can play. There was no disguising the fact that small-town politics, which had remained the principal school of character of the notables in every region, were now played out "beneath the boots": that is, they were subjected to constant intervention by the Roman governor, flanked by his military guard of honor, in the strong leather boots of the legionary. If the life

The deceased at the hunt, 4th century. A crew was needed to place the nets, hundreds of meters long (visible at the right). (Rome, Museum of the Conservators.)

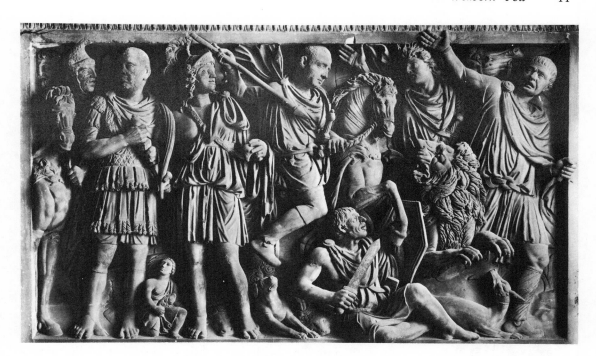

of the cities was to continue, the discipline and the solidarity of the local elites and their ability to control their own dependents had to be mobilized with greater self-consciousness than ever before. A sense of public discipline had to reach deeper into the private lives of the notables as the price for maintaining the status quo of an imperial order. Accordingly, a profound mutation in the attitude toward the married couple took place during the course of the second century A.D.

In the Late Republic and early Empire the womenfolk of public men had been treated as peripheral beings, who contributed little or nothing to the public character of their husbands. They were considered "little creatures," whose behavior and relations with their husbands were of no real concern to the all-male world of politicians. They might sap the characters of their males by sensuality; they might even inspire them to heroic improvidence through genuine love; they frequently emerged as strong resources of courage and good counsel in difficult times. But the married relationship in itself carried little weight on the public stage. Much of what we call the "emancipation" of women in upper-class Roman circles in the Early Empire had been a freedom born of contempt. The little creatures could do what they liked, as long as it did not

Sarcophagus, 3rd century. Mounted on a horse, the deceased, a cavalry officer, fights with a lion. Left, the officer again with one of his troops. Right, his men take part in a hunt. One of the army's official missions was to hunt wild animals, both to ensure the safety of the population and to capture animals for combats in the arena. Behind the officer, barebreasted, stands Valor. (Rome, Palazzo Mattei.)

Statue of a woman, based on an ancient Greek model, 1st or 2nd century. Note the majestic elegance of the pose and the robe. The left hand is veiled, for reasons of distinction, not modesty: in Greece it was considered elegant, even for orators, to leave the hands underneath one's clothing rather than to make grand gestures. The right hand and face are modern restorations. (Rome, Vatican Museums.)

interfere with the serious play of male politics. Divorce was quick and simple; adultery, though it might unleash occasional savage revenge on wife and lover, in no way affected the husband's public standing.

In the age of the Antonines the sense of the relative neutrality of upper-class marriage arrangements collapsed. The *concordia,* the *homonoia,* of the good marriage was now brought forward (often as a conscious revival of the imagined discipline of the archaic Roman past) to act as a resonant new symbol of all other forms of social harmony. Where the coins celebrating the crucial Roman political and social virtue of concordia had previously shown male politicians joining their right hands in alliance, with Marcus Aurelius it is his own wife, Faustina the younger, who appears on the coins associated with concordia. Young couples in Ostia are expected to assemble to offer sacrifice, "by reason of the exceptional concord" of the imperial pair. A little earlier, in *Advice on Marriage,* Plutarch had described how the husband should use the skilled personal guidance associated with the philosopher to bring his young wife, still thought of as a kittenish little creature more interested in her partner's sexual vigor than in his philosophical gravity, into line with the public deportment of the upper-class male. Marriage was to be a victory of the *mission civilisatrice* of the deportment of the wellborn along the disorderly fringe of their own class: their womenfolk. The contours of public eminence were that much more sharply drawn by including even women in the charmed circle of upper-class excellence. As a result, the married couple came to appear in public as a miniature of civic order. The *eunoia,* the *sumpatheia,* and the *praotes* of the relations of husband and wife echoed the expectations of grave affability and unquestioning class loyalty with which the powerful man both lovingly embraced and firmly controlled his city.

The role of the philosopher and of the moral ideas generated in philosophical circles in the second century must be seen against the tense background of a need for closer solidarity among the upper classes and for more intimate means of control over their inferiors. The philosopher, "moral missionary" of the Roman world, claimed to address humanity as a whole. He was "the teacher and leader of men, in all things that are appropriate to men according to nature."[1] In reality, he was no such thing. He was the representative of a prestigious counterculture within the elite, and he originally addressed his elevating message to members of that elite.

Carthage, 1st century. Mother Earth or Italia. (Paris, Louvre.)

The philosopher had never seriously considered address-ing the masses. He had reveled in the high moral status that came from preaching to the unconvertible among his peers. Philosophers had attempted to persuade the self-confident rul-ers of the world to live up to their own codes; in so doing, they had urged them to look beyond the narrow confines of their immediate social horizons. In Stoic exhortation the upper-class man was urged to live according to the universal law of the *cosmos,* and to attempt to rise above the brittle particularities and hot passions of mere human society. Such preaching had the effect of adding qualifications, reserves, additional dimensions, even consciously paradoxical a fortiori elaborations to well-known moral codes; "also" and "even" recur with telltale frequency. The public man was to think of himself as a citizen not only of his city but "also" of the world. The confirmed bachelor philosopher was to feel that "even" he should recognize the new status accorded to marriage, "for such a union is beautiful." The married man was to expect "even" himself to shun infidelity to his wife—"no, *not even* [!] with his own maidservant . . . a thing which some people consider quite without blame, since a master is held to have it in his power to use his slaves as he wishes." Behind his public face the public man was to be aware that, apart from the expectations of his peers, his inner motives were known "also" to the still presence of his guardian spirit.

Mosaic at Piazza Armerina, first half of 4th century. These ladies, whose attire barely preserves their modesty, are featured in a spectacle intended to titillate.

As spokesman for the counterculture of the wellborn, the philosopher enjoyed a paradoxical position as both buffoon

Sarcophagus, 3rd century, found at Acilia. As Bernard Andreae has shown, this was the sarcophagus of a consul. The elderly man wearing a crown visible to his right stands for the Senate. He looks toward the consul and with a gesture of the hand invites him to inaugurate his consulate with a solemn procession. Hence the young man with shaved head who is dressed in a toga is the consul's son. He will march in the parade and one day follow in his father's footsteps. (Rome, Museum of the Baths.)

and "saint of culture." Though their works bulk large on the shelves of modern libraries, it is far from certain that such works rested in great numbers on the shelves of the public men of the philosophers' own times. Papyrus fragments found in Egypt show that it was Homer who remained the true "mirror of the soul" of the Greek gentleman; the *Iliad* and the *Odyssey* can be reconstructed many times over from the debris of the shelves of the notables throughout the whole length of our period. Of the philosophical moralists of the second and third centuries, not a fragment in papyrus has survived. Competitive, logic-chopping, hopelessly otherworldly, when not hypocrites, hiding lust and ambition beneath their coarse cloaks and long, shaggy beards, the philosophers were fair game for the scorn of the majority. Frescoes flanking the seats of a public toilet in Ostia show these philosophers, self-styled masters of the art of living, offering their seated clients stern, gnomic counsels on the correct manner of defecation!

Yet *verba volant, scripta manent*: the philosophers' preaching had only to be transferred from its original, highly specific and class-based context and placed among a different social group, with a different social experience and significantly different moral preoccupations, for the "even's" and "also's" of philosophical exhortations to the upper classes quietly to drop away. What the philosophers presented as further refinement, tentatively added to an ancient and inward-looking morality of the elite, became, in the hands of Christian teachers, the foundation for the construction of a whole new building that embraced all classes in its demands. Philosophical exhortations, originally addressed to upper-class readers by writers such as Plutarch and Musonius, were drawn upon by Christian guides of the soul such as Clement of Alexandria in the late second century and passed along to respectable urban tradesmen and artisans. Philosophical exhortations enabled Clement to present Christianity as a truly universalist morality, rooted in a new sense of the presence of God and the equality of all men before His Law.

Lateral face of sarcophagus, 2nd century. Socrates with a Muse. He is doing the talking; she is his friend rather than his inspiration. (Paris, Louvre.)

The surprisingly rapid democratization of the philosophers' upper-class counterculture by the leaders of the Christian church is the most profound single revolution of the late classical period. Anyone who reads Christian writings or studies Christian papyri (such as the texts found at Nag Hammadi) must realize that the works of the philosophers, though they may have been largely ignored by the average urban notable, had drifted down, through Christian preaching and Christian speculation, to form a deep sediment of moral notions current among thousands of humble persons. By the end of the third century they had been made available to the inhabitants of the major regions of the Mediterranean, in the languages current among the lower classes in those regions: Greek, Coptic, Syriac, and Latin. In order to understand how this could happen, we must go back in time a few centuries and consider a very different region: the Palestine of Jesus. Then we must retrace our steps through very different segments of Roman society, to follow the growth of the Christian churches from the mission of Saint Paul to the conversion of Constantine.

The Good Shepherd with his Pan's pipe leads a stray lamb into his paradise. This shepherd tended no earthly flock but watched over the dead in a bucolic Eden; birds emphasize the scene's idyllic nature. 3rd century. (Rome, vault of the Catacomb of Saint Priscilla.)

✺ Person and Group in Judaism and Early Christianity

To move from the elites of the age of the Antonines, in the second and early third centuries A.D., to the world of later Judaism, of the second century B.C. onward, is to leave behind a morality securely rooted in a sense of social distance and enter the world of an afflicted nation. The very survival of the group as a whole held the center of moral anxiety.

The continuance of the traditions of Israel, the continued loyalty of Jews to those traditions and to each other, was the common, central issue for Jewish figures as various as the followers of Jesus of Nazareth, Saint Paul, and the later rabbinic sages—not to mention the communal experiments of the Essenes and the Qumran community. Seldom in the history of the ancient world are we confronted with such an explicit sense of the need to mobilize the whole of the self in the service of a religious law, and of the concomitant need to mobilize to the full a sense of solidarity between the members of a threatened community.

"But now the righteous have been gathered,
and the prophets are fallen asleep,
and we also are gone from the land,
and Zion has been taken from us,
and we have nothing now save the Mighty One and His
  Law."[2]

Even more unique in ancient literature is the clear and persistent expression of the underside of this concern for loyalty and for solidarity, an unrelieved anxiety that the participants will fail to give the whole of themselves to so demanding a venture. For only by such total loyalty could the affliction of Israel be reversed:

"If, therefore, we direct and dispose our heart,
we shall receive everything that we have lost."

The "heart" upon which such great hope must turn became the object of profound and somber scrutiny. Much as engineers, faced with the sagging mass of a building, are driven to concentrate on the most minute flaws, to pay attention to hitherto unexamined crystalline structures in the metals that support it, so late Jewish writers came to peer intently into the human heart. Like engineers, again, concerned with the fatigue and breaking points of metals, they noted with particular precision and concern the "zones of negative privacy," those dangerous opacities in the heart that threatened to exclude the demands of God and of fellow Jews (or fellow Christians) upon the whole of the self.

What emerged from these centuries of anxious concern for the solidarity of a threatened group was a sharp negative sense of the private. What was most private in the individual, his or her most hidden feelings and motivations, those springs of action that remained impenetrable to the group, "the thoughts of the heart," were looked to with particular attention as the possible source of the tensions that threatened to cause fissures in the ideal solidarity of the religious community.

This was a distinctive model of the human being. The starting point was the heart, presented as a core of motivation, reflection, and imagined intentions, that should ideally be single, simple—translucent to the demands of God and its neighbors. The heart of course was more habitually observed to be double. The double-hearted cut themselves off from God and their neighbors by retiring into those treacherous zones of negative privacy that screened them from such demands. Hence the sharpened features of the relations of the Jew, and later of the Christian, to the supernatural world. Shielded by "negative privacy" from the eyes of men, the heart was held to be totally public to the gaze of God and His angels: "When one commits a transgression in secret, it is as though he has thrust aside the feet of the Divine Presence."[3]

In the first century A.D. this model was supported, if with widely varying degrees of urgency and abruptness, by the belief that through the action of God a social state presently governed by the abrasive opacities of double-heartedness would give way, among a true remnant of Israel, to a time of utter transparency to each other and to God. In such a true, redeemed community, the tensions of the "evil heart" would have been eliminated. Backed by a sharpened belief in the Last Days and the Last Judgment, this high hope affirmed that a

Ivory tablet, 5th or 6th century. Height: 7 inches. Christ offering benediction, surrounded by the twelve apostles and flanked by Saints Peter and Paul. The eight books in the box are the four Gospels and the four great prophets. The perspective is reversed: the foreground figures are smaller than the background ones. The rather harsh style is that of a copyist working from an unknown model. (Dijon, Museum of Fine Arts.)

Ivory in high relief. Height: 6 inches. Preaching of Saint Paul, or possibly of Saint Mark, legendary founder of the Church of Alexandria; here he may be surrounded by 35 of his successors as head of that church. If that assumption is correct, the work would date from 607–609, and the city would be Alexandria. (Paris, Louvre.)

state of total solidarity and of openness to others was the predestined and natural state of social man—a state lost in the sad course of history, but to be regained at the end of time. Many groups believed that the ideal conditions that would be achieved at the end of time might be foreshadowed in a present religious community. A group such as the early Christian community believed in the present coming of the Holy Spirit upon the true remnant of Israel. Its adherents could expect to experience, if in the hauntingly transient form of possession, those solemn moments when the "hidden things of the heart" would stand revealed, as the community of the "saints" stood undivided, their hearts unveiled, in the very presence of God.

This is the vision of solidarity and, consequently, of the total permeability of the private person to the demands of the religious community that came to haunt the ancient world in its last centuries.

When we talk of the rise of Christianity in the cities of the Mediterranean, we are speaking of the destiny of an exceptionally labile and structurally unstable fragment of sectarian Judaism. The mission of Saint Paul (from about A.D. 32 to about A.D. 60) and of similar apostles had consisted of gathering the Gentiles into a new Israel, made available to them at the end of time by the messiahship of Jesus. In practice, this new Israel was formed among pagans who had been attracted, with varying degrees of commitment, to the influential Jewish communities of the cities of Asia Minor and the Aegean and to the large Jewish community in Rome. In its view of itself, the new Israel was a "gathering in": Jesus, as Messiah, had broken down previous "walls of division." Paul in his letters recited the traditional catalogues of opposed groups of persons—Jew and Gentile, slave and freeman, Greek and barbarian, male and female—in order to declare that such categories had been eradicated within the new community. The sole initiation into the group—a single purificatory bath— was presented by Paul as a stripping away of the garments of all previous social and religious categories, and the putting on of Christ, by which Paul meant the gaining by each believer of a single, uncompartmented identity, common to all members of the community, as befitted "sons of God" newly adopted "in Christ."

This potent mirage of solidarity flickered on the horizons of bodies of men and women whose position in Roman society made the achievement of such solidarity a hope destined to remain forever unfulfilled and, for that reason, all the more poignantly central to their moral concerns. The early Christian converts lacked the social situation that would have made Paul's mighty ideal of undifferentiated solidarity "in Christ" possible. The patrons and disciples of Paul and his successors were not simple souls, nor were they the humble and oppressed of modern romantic imagination. Had they been so, his ideals might have been realized more easily. Rather, they were moderately wealthy and frequently well traveled. As a result, they were exposed to a range of social contacts, of opportunities for choice and hence for potential double- hearted conflict, on many more issues than were, for instance, the rural poor of the "Jesus Movement" of Palestine or the members of the sedentary and enclosed Jewish settlement at Qumran. To "follow Jesus" by moving from village to village in Palestine and Syria, to "choose the Law" by abandoning "the will of their own spirit" in a monastic grouping perched on the edge of the Judaean wilderness, exposed believers to a range of choices mercifully more restricted than those experienced by the men and women of the "gatherings of the saints" in large and prosperous cities such as Corinth, Ephesus, and Rome. In the history of the Christian churches in the first and second centuries A.D. we are looking along a rich vein of human material notably different from that known to us either among the wellborn of the cities or among the villagers of the Gospels.

We need look only at the Roman Christian community of around A.D. 120, as it is revealed in the visions collected in the *Shepherd* of Hermas, to see what this could mean. Here was a religious group where everything that a student of ancient religion could have predicted as capable of going wrong in a "Pauline" urban community had indeed gone wrong. Hermas was a prophet obsessed with preserving a single-hearted solidarity among the believers. He wished poignantly for a childlike innocence of guile, of ambition, of double-hearted anxiety among his community. Yet Hermas' fears reveal a group whose very sins were a measure of its

Detail of pagan sarcophagus, before A.D. 275. Many pagan sarcophagi represent images of paradise borrowed from early Christianity. (Rome, Museum of the Baths.)

success in society. The church in Rome was supported by rich patrons, whose contacts with the pagan community at large had provided protection and prestige. The hearts of the influential Christians were predictably divided between the demands of solidarity and open-hearted dealing among the faithful, and concern for the conduct of their business ventures (hence with their contacts with pagan friends). The wealth of their households and the success of their sons preoccupied them. Hermas had no doubt that such persons, though a source of anxiety and of double-hearted tension, played a crucial role in a well-to-do Christian community: they were the solid, dry wood over which the vine of a prosperous and highly articulate religious community scrambled abundantly.

The prophet himself, Hermas—"patient, not given to indignation, always with a smile"—was no simple soul. He was a successful and sophisticated slave in an urban household. He had been disturbed by sexual attraction for his mistress, who, though a good Christian woman, still expected Hermas, as her slave, to help her naked out of the Tiber after her bath! He had witnessed the ravages of guile and double-hearted dealings among rich Christian patrons, among priests, and among rival prophets. Yet he couched a large part of his message against the backdrop of a classical Arcadian idyll, for this denouncer of the double-hearted contagion of wealth experienced his visions in a well-trimmed little vineyard property, which he happened to own in the residential countryside just outside Rome! As Ortega y Gasset has said, the virtues we do not possess are those that mean most to us. Much of the history of the early Christian churches is the history of an urgent search for equilibrium among those whose ideal of single-hearted loyalty to each other and to Christ was constantly eroded by the objective complexity of their own position in Mediterranean society.

Early Christian Morality

Paul wrote the community at Corinth, possibly in the spring of A.D. 54: "God is not the author of confusion, but of peace, as in all the churches of the saints." As so often, Paul was writing to impose his own interpretation (in this particular case, to stress the need for prophecy in languages intelligible to all) on a situation of insoluble complexity. As we have seen, the Christian churches in the cities depended on respectable and well-to-do households, members of which might welcome certain rituals of undifferentiated solidarity. But life in

Arycanda (Lycia). In 311–312, a year before the triumph of Christianity, delegates from one province asked the emperor to make those "atheists," the Christians, stop violating the rules of piety. To that end, they were to be forbidden from engaging in their execrable practices and ordered to worship the gods. (Museum of Istanbul.)

an urban environment, unless lived permanently among the totally uprooted and marginal—which was not the case in the Christian urban communities of the first, second, and third centuries—could not be based upon such high moments. If singleness of heart was to survive in the Christian churches and be seen to survive before a suspicious pagan world on the relentlessly public stage of everyday life in the city, it could survive only if caught in the fixative of a group life consciously structured according to habitual and resilient norms.

Hence the paradox of the rise of Christianity as a moral force in the pagan world. The rise of Christianity altered profoundly the moral texture of the late Roman world. Yet in moral matters the Christian leaders made almost no innovations. What they did was more crucial. They created a new group, whose exceptional emphasis on solidarity in the face of its own inner tensions ensured that its members would practice what pagan and Jewish moralists had already begun to preach. That singleness of heart for which a man such as Hermas yearned would be achieved in the successful community of Rome less through the undifferentiated workings of the Spirit, than by the intimate discipline of a tight-knit group, whose basic moral attitudes differed from those of their pagan and Jewish neighbors only in the urgency with which such attitudes were adopted and put into practice.

It is important to note at the outset the crucial difference between the widespread morality adopted by the Christians and the codes of behavior current among the civic elites. Much of what is claimed as distinctively "Christian" in the morality of the early churches was in reality the distinctive morality of a different segment of Roman society from those we know from the literature of the wellborn.

It was a morality of the socially vulnerable. In modestly well-to-do households the mere show of power was not available to control one's slaves or womenfolk. As a result, concern for intimate order, for intimate restraints on behavior, for fidelity between spouses and obedience within the household acted out "in singleness of heart, fearing God," tended to be that much more acute. Obedience on the part of servants, fair dealings between partners, and the fidelity of spouses counted for far more among men more liable to be fatally injured by sexual infidelity, by trickery, and by the insubordination of their few household slaves than were the truly wealthy and powerful. Outside the household a sense of solidarity with a wider range of fellow city-dwellers had developed, in marked contrast to the civic notables, who continued throughout the period to view the world through the narrow slits of their traditional "civic" definition of the urban community. A sense of solidarity was a natural adjunct of a morality of the socially vulnerable. There was, therefore, nothing strange, much less specifically Christian, in the inscription on the undoubtedly pagan tomb of an immigrant Greek pearl merchant on Rome's Via Sacra: "[Here] lie contained the bones of a good man, a man of mercy, a lover of the poor."

Trajan cancels the tax debts of the poor. Date: under Trajan or Hadrian. Poor citizens (as shown by their clothing) deposit the tablets on which their debts are recorded so that they can be destroyed. (Rome, Forum; now in the Curia.)

A Morality of the Vulnerable

The difference in the attitudes of the upper classes and the average urban dweller toward giving and sharing affords a sharp contrast. The civic notables "nourished" their city; they were expected to spend large sums maintaining the sense of continued enjoyment and prestige of its regular citizens. If such nourishment happened to relieve some distress among the poor, this was considered an accidental byproduct of relief from which the civic body as a whole, the rich quite as much as the poor, benefited by virtue of being citizens. A large number of the city's inhabitants—most often the truly poor, such as slaves and immigrants—were excluded from such nourishment. These large sums were given to the city and its citizens to enhance the status of the civic body as a whole, not to alleviate any particular state of human affliction among the poor. Individual donations could be magnificent displays of fireworks celebrating great occasions—the power and generosity of the patrons, the splendor of the city. The idea of a steady flow of giving, in the form of alms, to a permanent category of afflicted, the poor, was beyond the horizon of such persons.

Among the socially vulnerable it was a matter of daily perception that a relationship did exist between the superfluity enjoyed by the modestly well-to-do and the lack of means experienced by their poorer neighbors. Such an imbalance could be remedied, or at least muted, by the redistribution of very small sums, such as were within the reach of any modest city household or of any comfortable farmer among the rural poor of the countryside. It had long been obvious also to the Jewish communities, as it would be to the Christians, that among small men the maintenance of a margin of financial independence in a hostile world was possible through a small measure of mutual support. By offering alms and the chance of employment to the poorer members of their community, Jews and Christians could protect correligionists from impoverishment, and hence from outright vulnerability to pagan creditors or pagan employers. It is against this social background that we can begin to understand how the practice of almsgiving to the poor soon became a token of the solidarity of threatened groups of believers. The eventual replacing of a model of urban society that had stressed the duty of the wellborn to nourish *their* city by one based on the notion of the implicit solidarity of the rich in the affliction of the poor remains one of the most clear examples of the shift from a classical to a postclassical Christianized world. This shift was under way by the second century A.D. among the Christian communities.

Even without the intervention of the Christian churches, we can detect the slow rise, alongside the civic codes of the notables, of a significantly different morality, based on a different world of social experience. By the early third century, long before the establishment of the Christian church, aspects of Roman law and of Roman family life were touched by a subtle change in the moral sensibilities of the silent majority of the provincials of the Empire. Respectable wedlock was extended to include even slaves. Emperors posed increasingly as guardians of private morality. Suicide, that proud assertion of the right of the wellborn to dispose, if need be, of his own life, came to be branded as an unnatural "derangement."

The Christian church caused this new morality to undergo a subtle process of change by rendering it more universal in its application and far more intimate in its effect of the private life of the believer. Among Christians a somber variant of popular morality facilitated the urgent search for new principles of solidarity that aimed to penetrate the individual ever more deeply with a sense of the gaze of God, with a fear of His Judgment, and with a sharp sense of commitment to the unity of the religious community.

To appreciate the extent of the changes in moral ideals brought about within the churches we need only consider the structures of marriage and sexual discipline that developed in Christian households during the course of the second and third centuries. Galen was struck by the sexual austerity of the Christian communities in the late second century: "Their contempt of death is patent to us every day, and likewise their restraint in cohabitation. For they include not only men but also women who refrain from cohabiting all their lives; and they also number individuals who, in self-discipline and self-control, have attained a pitch not inferior to that of genuine philosophers."[4]

On the surface the Christians practiced an austere sexual morality, easily recognizable and acclaimed by outsiders: total sexual renunciation by the few; marital concord between the spouses (such as had begun to permeate the public behavior of the elites, if for very different reasons); strong disapproval of remarriage. This surface was presented openly to outsiders. Lacking the clear ritual boundaries provided in Judaism by circumcision and dietary laws, Christians tended to make their exceptional sexual discipline bear the full burden of expressing the difference between themselves and the pagan world. The message of the Christian apologists was similar to that of later admirers of clerical celibacy, as described by Nietzsche. They appealed to "the faith that a person who is an exception on this point will be an exception in other respects as well."[5]

It is important to understand the new inner structures that supported what on the surface seemed no more than a dour morality, readily admired by the average man. The commonplace facts of sexual discipline were supported by a deeper structure of specifically Christian concerns. From Saint Paul onward, the married couple had been expected to bear in their own persons nothing less than an analogue in microcosm of the group's single-hearted solidarity. Even if these might be

The Democratization of Moral Codes: Sexual Behavior

Rome, bas-relief reused on Constantine's Arch. Marcus Aurelius distributes family allowances to needy citizens, not out of charity but in order to sustain the citizenry. The distinction between citizens and noncitizens was gradually giving way to a distinction between the upper class and the common folk. One inscription refers to "plebeians, free or unfree." In this relief, however, we see only citizens. The one in the center owned a toga, or ceremonial costume; the other two are dressed as plebeians. The woman wears the robe of the female citizen, which extends to the feet.

dangerously confused by the workings of the Holy Spirit, in the undifferentiated "gatherings of the saints" the proper relations of husbands and wives, of masters and slaves, were reasserted in no uncertain manner within the Christian household. These relations were invested with a sense that such fidelity and obedience manifested in a peculiarly transparent manner the prized ideal of unfeigned singleness of heart. With the moral gusto characteristic of a group that courted occasions on which to test its will to cohesion, Christian urban communities even abandoned the normal means which Jewish and pagan males had relied upon to discipline and satisfy their wives. They rejected divorce, and they viewed the remarriage of widows with disapproval. The reasons they came to give, often borrowed from the maxims of the philosophers, would have pleased Plutarch. This exceptional marital morality, practiced by modestly well-to-do men and women, betrayed an exceptional will for order: "A man who divorces his wife admits that he is not even able to govern a woman."[6]

It was quite possible for Christian communities to settle down into little more than that. Marital morality could have been presented as a particularly revealing manifestation of the will of the group to singleness of heart. Adultery and sexual scheming among married couples could have been presented as the privileged symptoms of the "zone of negative privacy" associated with doubleness of heart. Without the tolerant space accorded by the ancient city to the upper-class males in which to work off their adolescent urges in relatively free indulgence in sexuality, young people would have married early, as close to puberty as possible, in order to mitigate through lawful wedlock the disruptive tensions of sexual attraction. Women and, it was occasionally hoped, even men would be disciplined by early marriage and by a sense of the piercing gaze of God penetrating into the recesses of the bedchamber. By avoiding remarriage the community could assure for itself a constant supply of venerable widows and widowers able to devote time and energy to the service of the church. Less exposed than notables to the tensions associated with the exercise of real power—bribery, perjury, hypocrisy, violence, and anger— these quiet citizens "of the middling condition" could show their concern for order and cohesion in the more domestic sphere of sexual self-discipline.

The disturbing ease with which the sexes mingled at ritual gatherings of Christians remained distasteful to respectable pagans, and strangers avoided speaking to Christians for that reason. A Christian contemporary of Galen actually petitioned the governor of Alexandria for permission to allow himself to be castrated, for only by such means could he clear himself and his correligionists from the charge of promiscuity! On a more humble level, the difficulties in arranging matches for young people, especially for Christian girls, in a community

Detail of Christian sarcophagus, 5th century(?). The miracle of the loaves. (Rome, Museum of the Baths.)

anxious to avoid marriage with pagans ensured that issues of sexual control would be treated with an intensity greater than that of more settled communities. It also meant that the resulting morality would be much more apparent to outsiders and applied much more rigorously to believers.

From Control to Continence   Such pressures go a long way to explain the moral tone of the average late antique Christian community. What they cannot explain is the further revolution by which sexual renunciation—virginity from birth, or continence vowed at baptism, or continence adopted by married couples or widowers—became the basis of male leadership in the Christian church. In this, Christianity had made *il gran rifiuto* (the great renunciation). In the very centuries when the rabbinate rose to prominence in Judaism by accepting marriage as a near-compulsory criterion of the wise, the leaders of the Christian communities moved in the diametrically opposite direction: access to leadership became identified with near-compulsory celibacy. Seldom has a structure of power risen with such speed and sharpness of outline on the foundation of so intimate an act of renunciation. What Galen had perceived at the end of the second century would distinguish the Christian church in later centuries from both Judaism and Islam.

It is claimed that a disgust for the human body was already prevalent in the pagan world. It is then assumed that when the Christian church moved away from its Jewish roots, where optimistic attitudes toward sexuality and marriage as part of God's good creation had prevailed, Christians took on the bleaker colors of their pagan environment. Such a view is lopsided. The facile contrast between pagan pessimism and Jewish optimism overlooks the importance of sexual renunciation as a means to singleness of heart in the radical Judaism from which Christianity emerged. The possible origins of this renunciation may be diverse in the extreme, but they do not in themselves explain why sexual renunciation rapidly became a badge of specifically male leadership in the Christian communities of the second and third centuries.

We must ask not why the human body could have come to be treated with such disquiet in late antiquity, but the exact opposite. Why is the body singled out by being presented so consistently in sexual terms—as the locus of imagined recesses of sexual motivations and the center of social structures thought of sexually—as being formed originally by a fateful sexual drive to marriage and childbirth? Why was this particular constellation of perceptions about the body allowed to carry so huge a weight in early Christian circles? It is the intensity and the particularity of the charge of significance that counts, not the fact that this significance often was expressed in terms so harshly negative as to rivet the attention of the modern reader, who is understandably bruised by such language.

The division between Christianity and Judaism was sharpest in this. As the rabbis chose to present it, sexuality was an enduring adjunct of the personality. Though potentially unruly, it was amenable to restraint—much as women were both honored as necessary for the existence of Israel, and at the same time were kept from intruding on the serious business of male wisdom. It is a model based on the control and segregation of an irritating but necessary aspect of existence. Among the Christians the exact opposite occurred. Sexuality became a highly charged symbolic marker precisely because its disappearance in the committed individual was considered possible, and because this disappearance was thought to register, more significantly than any other human transformation, the qualities necessary for leadership in the religious community. The removal of sexuality—or, more humbly, removal from sexuality—stood for a state of unhesitating availability to God and one's fellows, associated with the ideal of the single-hearted person.

The Three Children of Israel, 7th–8th century. The arched doorways were for loading wood into the pyre. The Jews are wearing Phrygian caps because they were Orientals. (Verona, Crypt of Santa Maria.)

Fresco, 10th century. Pope Sylvester (314–355). This contemporary of Constantine witnessed the triumph of Christianity and the founding of Saint Peter's in Rome. (Rome, Museum of Saint Paul's Outside-the-Walls.)

⚘ Church and Leadership

THE rise of a celibate male leadership in the Christian church brings us to the reign of Constantine and beyond. From the earliest period, the many forms of this celibacy had a drive to create a firmly delineated "public" space in the midst of the loose confederation of households that made up the Christian community. This was public space created in the bodies of the leaders themselves. Celibacy, however entered into, for the Christian community meant removal from what was held to be one of the most private sources of motivation and the dismantling of one of the most private social bonds on which the continuity and the cohesion of normal society depended. Its effect was to place the society of the Church, ruled and represented in public by celibate males, over against the society of the world, in which double-hearted pride, ambition, and the stubborn solidarities of family and kin group raged unchecked.

Such celibacy tended to take the form of postmarital abstinence from sexual relations. It was usually adopted in middle age and would later be imposed on priests after the age of thirty. This form of celibacy came to be expected as the norm for the average urban clergyman in the late antique period. It was not a spectacular renunciation. Sexuality was considered by ancient men to be a volatile substance, rapidly used up in the "heats" of youth. The grim facts of mortality in an ancient society ensured a constant supply of serious-minded widowers, who were available by their early middle age, "all passion spent," free to indulge in the more public joys of clerical office. In such a way celibacy demarcated quite unmistakably the existence of a class of persons who were central to the public life of the church, precisely because they were permanently removed from what was considered most private in the life

Gold medallion, ca. A.D. 330. Constantine and his imaginary companion, Alexander the Great. An autocrat who had one of his sons and one of his wives put to death, Constantine assumed the role of head of the Catholic Church. On the eve of their victory, the Christians were a minority, but an active and concentrated one.

of the average Christian layman in the world. Incorrectly remembering Hermas' *Shepherd* a hundred years later, Origen would speak of the "married," no longer simply of the rich, as the solid, unproductive wood over which vine of the church scrambled.

Celibacy, in the strict sense of entering into a state of permanent sexual abstinence, was unusual for public men in the Roman world. Thinking of himself as a man in his prime, whose social status gave him unthinking access to sexual satisfaction, Augustine admitted in Milan that, for all the high influence and access to the great that he envied in Ambrose, the Christian bishop, "his celibate state seemed a most hard thing to endure." For active men to come to create a "public" space in their own bodies through the renunciation of marriage, such public space had to be palpable (even attractive) and the community's need for a public space defined in this drastic manner, in the persons of its leaders, had to be very urgent indeed.

This was certainly the case for the Christian church of the third century. By A.D. 300 this church had become a public body in all but name. In 248 the church of Rome had a staff of 155 clergy and supported some fifteen hundred widows and poor. Such a group, quite apart from the regular congregation, was as large as the city's largest trade association. It was an enormous assemblage in a city where the average cult-group or burial club could be numbered in scores, not in hundreds. More revealing, perhaps, Pope Cornelius had paraded these impressive statistics as part of his claim to be regarded as the legitimate bishop of the city. Cyprian, who supported him, was careful to stress the "moral delicacy of virginal continence" with which Cornelius had shrunk from seizing high office. With such impressive responsibilities and resources at stake in every major city of the Empire, celibacy and the language of power had to be seen as one on the wider stage of Roman urban life. By being celibate and detached from the world in this manner, by the end of the third century the Christian bishops and clergy had become an elite equal in prestige, in the eyes of their admirers, to that of the traditional elites of urban notables.

It is to such a church, now firmly controlled by such leaders, that the conversion of the emperor Constantine, in 312, gave a fully public standing that proved decisive and irreversible in the course of the fourth century.

Glass on gold, Christian era. A family heirloom with no religious overtones; the sumptuously costumed couple receive victors' crowns, an omen of prosperity.

The empire that Constantine ruled as a declared Christian, from 312 to 337, was profoundly different from the classical urban society of the age of the Antonines. The huge fact of world-empire, present from the very beginning, finally was brought home to the cities. After 230 perceptible increases in taxation were necessary to maintain the unity and defense of the empire. In ancient conditions such increases meant far more than an increase in the proportion of the surplus appropriated by the imperial government. Upper-class society itself

Empire and City after
A.D. 300

Mausoleum, 3rd century. Images of wealth. Above: noble leisure (the master returns from a rabbit hunt). Below: running the estate (the master consults the account book in the presence of his paymaster and a sharecropper). (Trier, Landesmuseum.)

Ivory Diptych (right-hand portion), ca. A.D. 400; height: 12 inches. When a noble was awarded a high-ranking position, he had the fact recorded on an ivory tablet. Above, Rufius Probianus, named vice-prefect (of Rome?), sits on a throne, flanked by secretaries. With his hand he makes the "orator's gesture," which indicates that he is speaking, or that he has the right to speak, while others only have the right to listen. Below, two well-dressed lawyers (one holds a petition in his hand) raise their hands to beg the official's attention, as schoolchildren do in class and as the Greeks did to attract the attention of a god. (Berlin, Staatsbibliothek.)

had to be restructured so as to gain unimpeded access to that surplus. Old-fashioned local exemptions and the old-fashioned reluctance to injure the status of the rich by direct taxation were set aside. Direct intervention in the affairs of the cities became the norm for the imperial administration.

Such taxation did not cause the cities to disappear; still less did it eliminate the traditional elites. The elites merely changed their structure. Those who now wished to dominate society did so by combining their former positions as local notables with new roles as servants of the emperor. With the towering advantages of access to the imperial administration behind them, they came to consider themselves that much less fellow citizens, competing with a circle of equals in the traditional manner to nourish their "most sweet city." They were the *potentes,* the men of power, who controlled their cities in the name of the distant emperor in a manner that was far more blatant and much less sensitive to the delicate restraints of the diffused peer group of the wellborn. We noted in the age of the Antonines the enormous pressure brought to bear on the average civic notable by the insistence on a shared culture, and especially on a shared morality of social distance. By emphasizing the unbridgeable differences between their own class and everyone else, the Antonine wellborn had been able to consider themselves part of a group of interchangeable members of an elite. In the second and early third centuries this emphasis had effectively masked growing inequalities among the upper classes and the outright dominance within the upper class of those whose status depended on the service of the emperor. By the end of the third century these facts came to be accepted as the basic pattern on which Roman society had to be organized, if it was to survive. The later Roman Empire was a society explicitly dominated by an alliance of the servants of the emperor and of great landowners, who collaborated to control the taxpaying peasants and to assert law and order in the cities. The dominance of the few at the expense of their wellborn peers was stated unambiguously by the potentes of the reign of Constantine and his successors. Codes of behavior for the public man changed dramatically. Viewed by the sober eyes of men who liked to remember the older codes, the public man as *potens* came to blossom indecently. The discreet, uniform dress of the classical period, common to all members of the upper classes (think of the toga, heavy with overtones of the unchallenged dominance of a class of interchangeable *nobiles*) was abandoned in favor of the use of dress as a heraldry, designed to show hierarchical divisions within the upper classes. These new robes ranged from the billowing silk gowns of senators and the uniform-based dress of the imperial servants, embroidered with panels that indicated precise official ranks, to the studiously faceless tunic affected, in an equally explicit manner, by the Christian bishop. Previously it had been the body itself, its deportment in public and frequently, in the public baths, in the nude, that had given the most clear signals of natural membership of a distinctive class. Now the body was swathed in its owner's rank, in the form of heavy, close-fitting dress, each of whose ornaments spoke explicitly of a position in a hierarchy that culminated at the imperial court.

As for the city, in most regions of the Empire economic conditions ensured that it would no longer be an expanding site, a stage on which the competitive urges of the notables could express themselves in ever more lavish buildings, spectacles, and forms of public largesse. These aspects of the city did not vanish, however. They were maintained, often splendidly, in the great imperial residences at Trier, Sirmium, and, above all, Constantinople, as well as in major cities such as Rome, Carthage, Antioch, Alexandria, and Ephesus. But the splendor of the cities was now maintained by the Emperor, and on his behalf by the potentes. From being a vivid stage for the deployment of local energies in its own right, the city had become instead a microcosm of the ordered security of the Empire as a whole.

The fourth-century city was no pale shadow of its classical past. Much of its public decor had been carefully maintained, including the imposing facades of old pagan temples. In a surprising number of cities the imperial government continued to provide a privileged supply of foodstuffs, access to which was strictly limited, as in previous centuries, to citizens, irrespective of personal wealth or poverty. Similar supervision maintained vast public baths in all major cities. The circus, the theater (many altered at this time to accommodate ever more grandiose displays, such as water battles and wild beast hunts), and, most notoriously in Constantinople, the hippodrome replaced the ancient spaces traditionally associated with pagan public worship as the places where the loyalty of the city to its rulers, and so to its own survival, was solemnly expressed. The numinous associations attached to the proper performance of serious ceremonies clustered around such gatherings with as much intensity as in the religious ceremonies of pagan times. In Trier, Carthage, and Rome—all menaced and mauled by barbarians in the fifth century—the populace remained convinced that the performance of solemn circus games had effected, through their mysterious occult power, the continued survival of their city.

The potentes appeared less frequently in the forum. They now tended to dominate their cities from opulent palaces and country villas, set a little apart from traditional centers of public life. Rather than retreats from public life, however, these residences were the forum made private. The private rooms of the women's quarters were flanked by large halls for ceremonial receptions, often with an apse at one end. The small banquets held here were solemn gatherings of the inner group that ruled the city, very different from the magnificently indiscriminate civic banquets of clients, freedmen, friends, and fellow citizens on which, three centuries before, the younger Pliny had lavished his supplies of studiously indifferent cheap wine. Many of the masterpieces of classical statuary that once had stood in or around the temples and the forums came to rest in the extensive courtyards and entry halls of such palaces. They were tokens of the right of the potentes to absorb and preserve, on their own terms, the best of the classical city. Such men and their dependents would have to be persuaded that the Christian bishop and his fast-growing religious community could offer an alternative to their own vision of an urban world restored and maintained through the frank exercise of their own power and that of their master, the emperor. It was far from certain in the course of the fourth century that the new Christian church could impose its own peculiar notions of community on the ancient city in this, the last, carefully restored stage of its long existence.

Church and City in the Fourth Century

The Christian bishop and his church were only one element in the new urban scene. Many churches might be magnificently constructed through imperial gifts, according to a new imperial design. The basilica was a building with heavy associations of the audience hall of the Emperor—and so of the judgment seat of God, invisible emperor of the world. The clergy might receive exemptions and privileged allocations of food. The bishop had access to the governors and the potentes, in intervening, above all, for the poor and oppressed. (Although, Augustine remarked, he often was kept waiting for hours on end in the entrance hall of the great, while more

important figures were admitted ahead of him.) Impressive
though the fourth-century church might have appeared, it was
marginal to the *saeculum,* a world whose main structures had
evolved beneath the huge ancient pressures of power and the
need for security and hierarchy. Christianity, even though now
the nominal faith of the powerful, was peripheral to that
saeculum.

The Christian community remained united by its distinctive mirage of solidarity. This solidarity could now be expressed in full public view by the ceremonies that took place
in the basilica of the bishop. Though no longer a "gathering
of the saints," the Christian basilica remained a place where
the structures of the saeculum were pointedly absent. Secular
hierarchy was less clear within the basilica than in the city
streets. For all the new prominence of the clergy, for all the
careful segregation of men and women (on most occasions
onto different sides of the basilica's great aisles), for all the
continued ability of the powerful to shine among the drab
mass of their inferiors in spectacular Sunday clothes (now
piously embroidered with scenes from the Gospels)—the
Christian basilica remained the scene of a coming together of
men and women of all classes, equally exposed, beneath the
high chair of the bishop in the apse, to the searching eye of
God. John Chrysostom made himself exquisitely unpopular
in Constantinople by his habit of following with his eyes
individual great landowners and courtiers as they strode in
and out of the basilica during his sermons, marking them out
by such a penetrating and public glance as the actual perpetra-
tors of the sins and social wrongs he was denouncing. The
old freedom of speech of the philosopher as critic of the great
was now brought to bear on an entire urban community,
gathered by its clergy into the audience hall of God. A community led in this manner, by such persons, was bound to
attempt to transform the ancient city into a community shaped
in its own, largely unfamiliar image.

In the eyes of these leaders the church was a new public
community held together by repeated emphasis on three
themes, each of which received a sharpness of focus hitherto
lacking in the ancient world: sin, poverty, and death. Those
three dark, seemingly faceless notions, closely interlocked,
ringed the horizon of the late antique Christian. Only by
coping with them in a manner laid down in no uncertain
manner by the clergy could the average man or woman gain
that "city of God" whose palpable joys still speak to a modern

Fragment of an engraved cup,
4th century. In front of the
viewing stand, a chariot rounds
a marker with three staffs and
balls. (Trier, Landesmuseum.)

So-called Temple of Bacchus at
Baalbek, mid-2nd century. This
temple, with its high foundation, is Roman in type, but the
columns are exceptionally tall.
The architecture of Roman
Syria is notable for its large
scale, its splendor, and (except
for Palmyra) its originality.

visitor in the sheer sensual delight of late antique Christian mosaics and in the stilled, ever-beautiful faces of the saints. For on the mosaics they could see the saints—men and women acceptable to God and placed by Him, not in some ethereal and antiseptic afterlife but in the ancient "Paradise of delights," in "a grassy place by refreshing waters, whence pain and suffering and groaning are fled."[7]

Sin and Community

The Christian basilica housed a gathering of sinners equal in their need for the mercy of God. The firmest boundaries within the group were those drawn by sin. One should not underestimate the element of novelty in such a definition of the community. Matters that might be as deeply private to the individual as his or her sexual mores or his or her opinions on Christian dogma could be adjudged by members of the clergy as grounds for a resounding public act of exclusion from the church. A public system of penance remained current throughout the period. Excommunication involved public exclusion from the Eucharist, and its effects could be reversed only by an equally public act of reconciliation with the bishop. Thus, in a fourth-century basilica public solidarity was linked to the issue of sin and to the even more interesting "thought crime" of heresy with a clarity that would be blurred in later ages. Access to the Eucharist involved a series of visible acts of separation and adhesion. The unbaptized were shepherded out of the building when the main liturgy of the Eucharist began. The ceremony began with the gesture of the believers in bringing offerings to the altar-table. In the final solemn advance of the faithful to participate in the "Mystical Supper," the only fixed hierarchy within the Christian group was made clear: bishops and clergy first, then the continent of both sexes, and, last of all, the married laity. In a specially designated area at the very back of the basilica, furthest from the apse, stood the "penitents," those whose sins excluded them from active participation. Ideally humbled, dressed beneath their status, their beards unshaven, they waited in full public view for the public gesture of reconciliation with their bishop. Occasionally the hierarchy of the saeculum and the democracy of sin would clash, with memorable results: in Caesarea, Basil refused the offerings of the heretical emperor Valens; in Milan, Ambrose kept the emperor Theodosius among the penitents—the ruler of the world stripped of his robe and diadem—for having ordered the massacre of the people of Thessalonica.

The poor were ever-present. The crippled and indigent, vagrants, and immigrants from an often afflicted countryside, hordes of them squatted at the doors of the basilica and slept in the porticoes surrounding its outer courtyards. The poor were spoken of always in the plural. They were described in terms that bore no relation to the earlier classification of society into citizen and noncitizen. They were the faceless human refuse of the ancient economy. It is precisely this anonymous quality that brought them into sharp focus as the remedy for the sins of the more fortunate members of the Christian community. Alms to the poor were an essential part of the prolonged reparation of penitents and the normal remedy for lesser, venial sins—sins of idle, impure thoughts and of minor self-indulgence—that did not require public penance.

The abject condition of the poor carried a heavy charge of religious meaning. They stood for the state of the sinner, in daily need of the mercy of God. The symbolic equation of the poor with the afflicted sinner, abandoned by God, recurred insistently in the language of the Psalms that formed the backbone of the church liturgy, and especially of its ceremonies of penance. Without such symbolism the leap of empathy simply would not have occurred, by which the urban dweller, accus-

Solidarity and the Poor

Mosaic, 4th century. A noble has had one of his villas depicted here. Its central courtyard is surrounded by a long loggia flanked by two majestic towers. The facade of the main building is roofed by small concrete cupolas, like the Baths of the Hunt at Lepcis. (Tunis, Bardo Museum.)

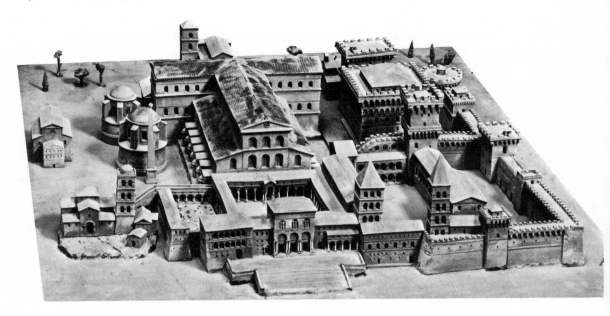

Marcelliani model of the medieval Vatican. The great edifice that is the left half of the model is the original Saint Peter's Basilica, construction of which was begun around 325. Every city had at least one "basilica," or official meeting hall, as did every palace.

tomed to perceiving such unpleasant human debris as little more than menacing exceptions to the rule of the ancient civic community of fellow citizens, came to accord to the poor a privileged status as symbols of the afflicted condition of mankind, his own sinful self included. Almsgiving became a potent analogue of the relation of God to sinful man. The whining of the beggars as the worshipers entered the basilica to pray were overtures of their own, desperate appeals to the mercy of God. "When thou art weary of praying," said John Chrysostom, "and dost not receive, consider how often thou hast heard a poor man calling, and hast not listened to him." "It is not for stretching out thy hand [in the *orans* gesture of prayer] that thou shalt be heard. Stretch forth thy hand not to heaven, but to the poor."[8]

The very anonymity of the poor helped maintain a sense of the undifferentiated solidarity of sinners in the church. The civic ideal that the great were under an obligation to give largesse pressed in upon the Christian church; for the civic ideal also implied that largesse made manifest the right of the powerful to control their community. After all, few basilicas would have been built without such a reflex. The most spectacular were gifts of the emperor or of leading clergymen. They were the acts of men who had every intention of making it clear, in the old-fashioned way, that they were the ones who had a right to nourish, and so to control, the Christian congregations who assembled in them. The names of those who brought offerings to the altar were read aloud in the solemn prayers of offering that preceded the Eucharist; frequently these names were acclaimed. Only the notion of sin could flatten the profile of so confident and high-pitched a pyramid of patronage and dependence. What the bishops emphasized, therefore, was the fact that every member of the Christian community had his or her own sins; and that, given as alms, any sum, however small, would be welcome to the truly poor. As a result, the obtrusive outlines of patronage by the great, expressed in stone, mosaic, silken hangings, and blazing candelabra, in the manner of the old civic munificence, were veiled in the slight, but steady drizzle of daily almsgiving by the sinful average Christian to the faceless afflicted.

The helplessness of the poor made them ideal clients for a group anxious to avoid the tensions caused by real relations of patronage to real clients. Of all the forms of patronage to which the clergy had long been exposed, the most perilous, and the most ignominious in the eyes of outsiders, was their dependence on wealthy women. From Cyprian onward, poverty and the role of influential women in the church were closely related. The wealth of many virgins, widows, and deaconesses created ties of patronage and of humiliating obligation between the clergy and women who, by the end of the fourth century, were leading members of the senatorial aristocracy. Such wealth, and the patronage associated with it, could be safely expended on the poor, for, as any ancient man knew, the poor could offer nothing in return; their support counted for nothing. Furthermore, strict codes of segregation between the sexes had blocked access by women to public power within the church. Any breach of these codes caused studiously nurtured scandal whenever there was a threat that influence in the church might come to be wielded by women on the strength of their wealth, culture, or superior courage. Such taboos, however, did not apply to a woman's public role as patroness of mere human wreckage. As patronesses of the poor, through almsgiving and through care of the sick and of the stranger in hostels, well-to-do women came to enjoy a real degree of public status in cities all over the Mediterranean that was exceedingly rare in any other aspect of the hierarchical, male-dominated public life of the powerful in the Late Empire.

As patron of the poor and protector of influential women,

The deceased Comminia, 4th or 5th century. This figure, in the Christian (and pagan) attitude of prayer, represents Comminia, her immortal soul, and prayer itself. (Naples, Catacombs of Saint January.)

Rome, tomb of a blacksmith
in the Catacomb of Saint
Domitilla, 4th–5th century.
The use of engraving, less
costly than relief, represents a
democratization of funerary art.
(Rome, Christian Museum of
the Lateran.)

whose energies and wealth he could direct into the service of
the church by acting as the spiritual director of large groups
of widows and virgins, the bishop rose to prominence in the
fourth-century city. He publicly associated himself with precisely those categories of persons whose existence had been
ignored by the ancient, "civic" model of the urban notables.
In the words of the *Canons of Saint Athanasius:* "A bishop that
loveth the poor, the same is rich, and the city, with its district,
shall honor him." One could not have asked for a more
pointed contrast to the civic self-image of the notables of two
centuries earlier.

The Christian community, growing up parallel to the
ancient city, though far from dominant within it in the fourth
century, had created through its public ceremonies its own
sense of a new form of public space, dominated by a new type
of public figure. Celibate bishops, largely supported by celibate women, based their prestige on the ability to nourish a
new category: the faceless, profoundly anticivic rootless and
abandoned poor. In the fifth century Mediterranean cities came
to be touched by further crisis. The crucial generations immediately preceding and following A.D. 400 were noted
equally for urban catastrophes, such as the sack of Rome by
the Visigoths in 410, and for the emergence of influential
bishops, such as Ambrose at Milan, Augustine at Hippo, Pope
Leo at Rome, Chrysostom at Constantinople, and Theophilus
at Alexandria. These bishops ensured that the restored facade
of the late Roman city would collapse upon itself, leaving the
Christian bishop with his noncivic definition of the commu-

Part of an ivory diptych; height: 12 inches. It commemorates the consulate of Flavius Felix in 426. He holds a scepter with an eagle on top as an insignia of his rank and wears a long tunic, a dalmatic on top, and over all, a sumptuously embroidered toga. We have moved from the age of draped garments to that of sewn garments with gold and silver embroidery. (Paris, Bibliothèque Nationale, Cabinet des Médailles.)

Funerary mosaic, 5th century(?). In Spain and Africa such mosaics cover the gravestone, almost level with the ground. Legible are the name of the deceased, his age, and the month and day of death but, as in this case, not always the year. The important thing was the date on which the anniversary of the death should be celebrated. (Tunis, Bardo Museum.)

nity free to act as the sole viable representative of urban life around the shores of the Mediterranean.

The Impact of the Afterlife

Outside the cities stretched the quieter final solidarity of the Christian graves. To walk from the pagan into the Christian rooms of any modern museum is to pass into a world of clear standard meanings. The haunting richness of the upper-class sarcophagi of the second and third centuries—over whose message scholars will long continue to labor, in large part because they are so resolutely idiosyncratic—gives way to a limited repertoire of clearly recognizable scenes, found with few variations on all Christian tombs. The amazing variety of pagan funerary inscriptions and pagan funerary art testifies to a society with few common meanings about death and the afterlife. The grave was a magnificently private place. The dead person, supported by his traditional groups—family, peer group, burial associates, even, in the case of the great, his city—had to make the meaning of his own death clear to the living. Hence the extraordinary proliferation of burial clubs among the humble, the crucial role of the family mausoleum among the well-to-do, and the almost bizarre diversity of the statements of the deceased or about the deceased. (Recall the Greek notable Opromoas, who covered his tomb with the letters of praise for his civic generosities, written about him by Roman governors, or the lines of a humble stoneworker, apologizing for the quality of the verses on his epitaph!) Such tombs are the joy of any reader of Greek or Latin epitaphs, but they are the despair of any historian of religion who might wish to elicit from them a coherent doctrine of the afterlife. In the pagan world of the second and third centuries no widespread religious community had intervened to muffle the variety of so many private voices from the grave.

With the rise of Christianity the church came gradually to intrude between individual, family, and city. The clergy claimed to be best able to preserve the memory of the dead; their Christian doctrine about the afterlife made clear to the living the meaning of the passing away of the deceased. Traditional graveside ceremonies continued to be performed, but they were not enough. Offerings at the Eucharist ensured that the names of the dead would be remembered in prayer in the Christian community as a whole, presented as the larger, artificial kin group of the believer. Annual feasts in memory of the dead and for the benefit of their souls—given, as always,

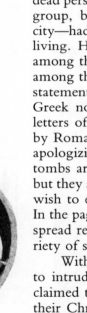

Detail of Christian sarcophagus, 4th century. For centuries funerary art showed husband and wife half turned toward each other, half toward the spectator. (Rome, Lateran Museum.)

to the ever-available poor—took place in the courtyards of the basilicas and even within their walls. The church rather than the city now made manifest the glory of the departed. Once brought within the precincts of the basilica, the democracy of sin was made to stretch beyond the grave in a manner inconceivable to pagans. The clergy could refuse the offering made on behalf of unconverted family members, of unrepentant sinners, and of suicides.

A new sense of holy ground drew the dead into the shadow of the basilicas. Large Christian cemeteries, administered by the clergy, had existed in Rome since early in the third century. They included carefully engineered subterranean galleries, designed to provide burial for the poor in great numbers. The graves of the poor, cut in ledges one above the other in the catacombs, remain to this day as silent witness of the clergy's determination to act as patrons of the poor. Even in death, the poor are mobilized. The rows of humble graves, placed at a decent distance from the mausoleums of the rich, represented the care and solidarity of the Christian community.

At the end of the fourth century the spread of the practice of *depositio ad sanctos,* the privilege of being buried in near proximity to the shrines of the martyrs, ensured that if the Christian community demanded a hierarchy of esteem among its members the clergy, who controlled access to such shrines, would emerge as the arbiters of that hierarchy. Virgins, monks, and clerics are buried closest to tombs of the martyrs in the cemeteries of Rome, Milan, and elsewhere. These, the new elites of the urban church, are followed by the humble laity, rewarded for good Christian behavior: "Probilianus . . . for Hilaritas, a woman whose chastity and good nature was known to all the neighbors . . . She remained chaste for eight years in my absence, and so she lies in this holy place."[9]

The dead, absorbed into the Christian churches in this highly visible manner, were imperceptibly removed from their city. In order to establish the repose and continued renown of their dead, the Christian family dealt only with the clergy. Civic forms of testimony were disregarded. Only among the old-fashioned in small Italian towns was the anniversary of a public figure still made the occasion of a large public civic banquet for the notables and their fellow citizens. Petronius Probus, greatest of the fourth-century Roman potentes, was mourned publicly by the imperial court as a "first citizen." But after that his memory was entrusted to the shrine of Saint

Statuette of an empress, ca. 380(?). The polished appearance results from more than just the use of marble and the illusion of scale. Under the cloak, folded in the Hellenistic manner, we glimpse the long, gold-embroidered scarf worn by empresses as early as the 3rd century. (Paris, Bibliothèque Nationale, Cabinet des Médailles.)

Painting from an imperial reception hall, before 326. The
aureole or nimbus indicates a
princess, or perhaps an alle-
gory; crowned with laurels, the
woman is showing her jewels
as a sign of prosperity. (Trier,
Episcopal Museum.)

Mosaic, portrait of Saint
Ambrose, 5th century. Here we
see the melancholy man of action, a small, aloof, cultivated
man whom Saint Augustine
managed to see only in church
on Sundays, a bishop whose
policy relied on acts of violence
calculated to look like caprices.
(Milan, Church of Saint
Ambrose.)

Peter. His splendid marble sarcophagus proclaimed Probus'
new intimacy with Christ in the court of Heaven. And so the
great man lay, some yards from Saint Peter himself, until
sixteenth-century workmen found his sarcophagus, filled with
the strands of gold woven into his last robe. As for the clergy

and other holy dead, the mosaics show them far from the ancient city. They tread the enamel-green grass of God's Paradise, beneath the Eastern palms, surrounded by a most unclassical group of peers: "and now among the Patriarchs [he lives], among the Prophets of clear future sight, among the Apostolic company, and with the Martyrs, mighty men of power."

Rome, Santa Maria Maggiore, ca. 435. Only the floor, the baldachin, and the altar are recent; the ceiling imitates the ancient style. With a grace more imperial than sacred, it could pass for a pagan civil basilica. This is a masterpiece in the antique style, with its harmonious precision of proportions. A frame in relief once surrounded each mosaic, between the columns and the windows; these reliefs varied the flatness of the upper sections without cutting them in two by interposing a continuous horizontal projection.

✃ The Challenge of the Desert

T HE rise of monasticism in the course of the fourth century brought a new element into the moral and social attitudes of the late antique Christian world. Constantine on one occasion wrote Saint Anthony, older than the emperor by almost a generation. Anthony, who had abandoned his village in the Fayum the year the emperor was born and was long settled in the outer desert of Egypt, was unimpressed. Pachomius, too, had established his first monasteries some years before Constantine became emperor in the East. The Constantinian dispensation, so notable in the cities, was a recent phenomenon compared to the world of the ascetics. The monks—*monachoi,* or "lonely ones"—drew on a very different, almost archaic, Christian tradition. Their spiritual and moral attitudes were nourished by the experience of a predominantly rural environment, very different from that of the urban Christians. In the fourth century the monks of Egypt and Syria enjoyed a *succès d'estime et de scandale* throughout the Mediterranean world. Athanasius' *Life of Anthony* appeared immediately after that saint's death in 356. Between 380 and 383 John Chrysostom withdrew, for a short but formative period, to live among the ascetics in the hills outside Antioch. "Journey in thought to the mountaintop on which Christ was transformed" remained the poignant dream of that most city-bound of Christian rhetors. In August 386 the story of Saint Anthony shocked Augustine out of his desire to marry and launched him on a trajectory that within a few years would lead to his ordination as bishop of Hippo, where he remained for the remaining thirty-five years of his life. By the end of the fourth century the role of the Christian church in the cities had been overshadowed by a radical new model of human nature and human society created by the "men of the desert."

Saint Paul the Simple.
Menology of Basil II, 11th century. (Rome, Vatican Library.)

The prestige of the monk lay in the fact that he was the
"lonely one." He personified the ancient ideal of singleness of
heart. He had renounced the world in the most starkly visible
manner possible. By an act of *anachôrésis,* he had moved away
to live in the desert: he was an anchorite, a man defined by
this single elemental move. Individual hermits or groups of
hermits settled on the tracts of useless (though by no means
always hostile) land that flanked the towns and villages of the
Near East. They were known as the men of the *erémos,* of the
desert, our "hermits." This desert had always been the ever-
present antithesis of the life of the settled world. Those who
moved into it often remained within sight and walking distance of the settled communities that they had abandoned;
they soon came to serve the villagers as heroes and spiritual
guides.

The monks moved in a marginal zone, clearly perceived
as shorn of the habitual supports and definitions of organized
life in society. They had settled on the social equivalent of an
Antarctic continent, reckoned from time immemorial to be a
blank space on the map of Mediterranean society—a no-man's-
land that flanked the life of the city, flouted organized culture,
and held up a permanent alternative to the crowded and relentlessly disciplined life of the villages.

In doing this, the individual monk had set himself free to
achieve, in the face of God and among his fellows, the ideal
of singleness of heart. Unriven by the tensions of settled so-

ciety, slowly and painfully purged of the murmurous promptings of demons, the monk longed to possess "the heart of the
righteous," a heart as unfissured, as clear of the knotted grain
of private, doublehearted motivation, as the solid, milk-white
heart of the date palm.

Admirers did not doubt that the monk, as "lonely one,"
had recaptured a touch of the original majesty of man. Centuries of speculation about the "glory of Adam" gathered
around his person. He stood, as Adam had stood, in single-
hearted worship of God in Paradise. The bleak, asocial land-
scape of the desert was a distant image of Paradise—the first,
the true home of humankind, where Adam and Eve had dwelt
in full majesty, before the subtle and overpowering onset of
the doublehearted cares of human life in settled society, before
marriage, physical greed, the labor of the earth, and the grind-
ing cares of present human society robbed them of their original serenity. Totally singlehearted, therefore joined with the
angelic hosts in unfailing and undivided praise of God, the life
of the monk mirrored on earth the life of the angels. He was
an "angelic man": "Often He showed me [said old man A-
nouph] the hosts of angels that stand before Him; often I have
beheld the glorious company of the righteous, the martyrs
and the monks—such as had no purpose but to honor and
praise God in singleness of heart."[10]

The monastic paradigm drew on the more radical aspects
of the pagan philosophic counterculture, most notably on the
magnificently asocial lifestyle of the Cynics, and on a long
Judeo-Christian past. Its originality lay in its dramatic shift of
viewpoint. It equated the world with a clearly identifiable
phenomenon—settled society as it existed in the present—and
it viewed that society as transparent to a sense of the true, that
is, of the "angelic," ordering of man's first estate. Behind the
preaching of a man such as John Chrysostom, in his sermons
around 382 *On Virginity,* we can sense the excitement of John's
monastic vision of a human race standing on the threshold of
a new age. The life of a city such as Antioch, the facts of
sexuality, of marriage, of childbirth, solid and immemorial as
they might seem, even to conventional Christians, appear now
as no more than a confused eddy in a stream that was slipping
fast from Paradise toward the Resurrection. Society, like human nature as adjusted to its demands, was an unplanned and
impermanent accident of history. "The present time draws to
its close; the things of the resurrection now stand at the
door."[11] All human structures, all human society—all "arts and

Detail of floor mosaic, 4th century. Not, as the guides would
have it, the devil sticking out
his tongue, but a cool Wind,
which complements the other
symbols of paradise visible in
the mosaic: flowers, river, and
a brimming pitcher. (Aquileia,
Cathedral.)

buildings," "cities and households"—even the socal definition of men and women as sexual beings destined for marriage and reproduction, were soon to come to rest in the vast hush of the presence of God. Those who had adopted the life of the monks and virgins on the edge of the city had anticipated the dawn of man's true nature; they were "ready to receive the Lord of Angels." That moment of rapt adoration at the high moment of the liturgy of the Eucharist (as celebrated in Antioch), when the faithful joined their voices with those of the angels in chanting "Holy, Holy, Holy" to the King of Kings as He approached unseen to the altar, revealed for an instant the true, undivided state of man. City, marriage, and culture, the "necessary superfluities" of settled life, were but a passing interlude compared with that clear state, shorn of the "cares of this life." The monks on the hills outside the city strove to make that moment last for a lifetime.

Desert and Society

Christian monasticism aimed to create a world stripped of familiar structures. The compartmentations, the hierarchies, the sharp distinctions on which the life of the city continued to be based, had been blurred and softened, by the impressive communal rituals within the Christian basilicas. But these basilicas remained encapsulated spaces within the solid structures of the city. Social structures might be held in suspense at high moments, but they were never banished entirely from the minds of the believers, who would step out of the basilica, once the ceremonies were over, to find themselves in the hard world of the late antique city. Men like John Chrysostom now wished all these to vanish in the growing radiance of a new age. The dawn light of the "things of the Resurrection" already played on the little settlements of "angelic men" on the hills around Antioch; it might slip down to bathe the sleeping city. This was Chrysostom's lifelong dream. He died in 407, in exile—broken by the power of the world. Yet the acceptance of monasticism by so many leading Christian figures betrayed a sense of the vulnerability of the cities, as these had been restored in the generation of Constantine. The fifth century was marked by barbarian invasion in the West and dogged organization of rising population and a consequent rising misery in the East. The newly created structures of the late Roman cities were yet further weakened as the radical monastic view of the world helped the articulate leaders of the Christian community to make plain the demise of the classical

city. The monks and their admirers were the first Christians of the Mediterranean to look beyond the ancient city. The monks saw a new society. Their personal preoccupation with new forms of personal discipline, which included the renunciation of sexuality, ensured that a very different flavor would be instilled into the private life of the Christian family within that society.

Coptic monastery of Saint Simeon, west of Aswan, in the desert. Cells are clustered inside a fortified wall. Founded in the 4th century, the building shown here is the result of 15 centuries of additions and modifications.

In the monastic paradigm the city itself lost its identity as a distinctive cultural and social unit. In many parts of the Near East the rise of the monks marked the end of the splendid isolation of the Hellenistic city from its surrounding countryside. City-dwellers who trooped out to seek the counsel and blessing of the holy men established in the neighborhood tended to meet there village illiterates, who could speak, at best, pidgin Greek. Throughout the Mediterranean region the monks joined the faceless poor in forming a new universal class, without ties to city or countryside because equally dependent on the mercy of God in either. The symbolism of the poor as dark mirrors of the abject condition of man was immensely heightened by little colonies of voluntary poor, which flanked the cities. The actual poor did not benefit, for

City and Countryside

Vaticanus latinus 1202, 11th century: An example of the lewdness which Saint Benedict of Norcia saw in Rome and which induced this Umbrian influenced by eastern monasticism to leave that city. He retired at first to Subiaco, to the ruins of the villa built by Nero in a beautiful rural setting. Later he founded the famous Monastery of Monte Cassino. The naked Venuses that were celebrated in ivory and silver as late as the 6th century here represent sin.

the laity preferred to give alms to the monks, the "ceremonial poor," whose prayers were known to be effective, rather than to the noisy and repulsive beggars surrounding the basilicas. The monks functioned much as a chemical solution functions in a photographer's darkroom: their presence brought out with greater sharpness of contrast the new features of a Christian image of society. This was an image that ignored the cities, by ignoring the old divisions of town and countryside, citizen and noncitizen, and concentrated on the universal division of rich and poor in town and countryside alike.

Take, for example, the Egyptian provincial city of Oxyrhynchus, which until the end of the third century had enjoyed a privileged supply of food. This supply was allotted to those who, irrespective of wealth or poverty, could claim descent from the citizen class, and the genealogies recorded to establish these claims go back to the very beginnings of the Roman urban order in Egypt. By the end of the fourth century, however, the city was ringed around with populous monasteries and convents, and the ancient structures had been definitively eclipsed. As Christians, the notables now competed to lavish charity on the poor and the strangers rather than on "the most resplendent city" of Oxyrhynchus.

The Christian notable is now the *philoptôchos,* "lover of the poor," no longer the *philopatris,* "lover of his home town"—though it is still on bended knee that the humble man must approach him. Although the misery of the poor had been revealed by Christian symbolism of sin and its reparation, they had not gone away. They shivered in the cold desert nights, as they crowded around the basilica for a Sunday meal, provided now by the monks, "on behalf of the souls" of the "most resplendent families," who still controlled the city of Oxyrhynchus and the surrounding countryside. These families no longer felt the need to express any special love for their city, as if it were any different from the mass of humble persons, whom they controlled in town and country alike. As "lovers of the poor," the great patronized the afflicted equally, whether they had been born in the city or in the countryside.

A New Education

Monasticism not only destroyed the particularity of the city; it threatened to weaken the city's hold on its notables at one of its most intimate points: it challenged the role of the public spaces of the city as the principal locus for the socialization of young males. It would be misleading to treat the

monks as if they were without exception illiterate heroes of an anticulture. Many converts to asceticism were educated men, who had found in the desert—or in the idea of the desert—a simplicity on the other side of great sophistication. In the hands of a Basil of Caesarea or an Evagrius of Pontus, techniques of moral grooming, standards of deportment and of spiritual discipline, previously practiced only by the elites of the cities, flowered with new vigor in the monasteries.

Nor was such a culture for mature men only; by the middle of the fourth century monastic settlements were being recruited from among the very young. Quite well-to-do village and urban families dedicated their children to the service of God, as often as not to keep the family heritage together, unburdened by excessive sons—and especially by surplus daughters. These very young monks did not simply vanish into the desert. They tended to reappear some years later, and even in the cities, as members of a new elite of abbots and clergymen of ascetic training. The monastery, therefore, was the first community prepared to offer a fully Christian training from boyhood up. The monks demanded that their young hermits absorb a literary culture based entirely on the liturgy and the Bible. Monastic practice sharpened existing codes of behavior, by basing the formation of young boys and girls on the slow penetration of their souls with dread "certainty of the Presence of the Invisible God." In its content and, even more, in the emotions to which it appealed, this process of socialization, as advocated in ascetic circles, spelled the end of

Codex Sinopensis on purple leaves, 6th century. In this case the decline of ancient academicism resulted in something other than clumsiness or naiveté: a lively theatrical talent is evident. At right is the prison where John the Baptist has just lost his head (the scene is agitated, and it is clear that a deed has just been done). At left, the head is brought to Herod Antipas, Herodiad, and Salome (wearing wigs), in the midst of a banquet. (Paris, Bibliothèque Nationale.)

the ideal of education by the city. For until the end of the fourth century it had been taken for granted that all boys, pagan and Christian alike, should be exposed to the magnificently noisy, articulate, and extroverted "shame culture" of competing peers, associated with the ancient rhetor's classroom on the edge of the forum. Now this could fall silent.

That so drastic a new model of education had so little effect on the public grooming of the younger members of the upper classes in this period is a telling symptom of the vigor of the late antique city. The educational ideals of the city were by no means absorbed by those of the monastery. Yet the monasteries clearly revealed a fissure that might open up at any later time between the city and the Christian households within it. The ancient city, whose intimate disciplines had molded the private and public identities of its upper-class members for centuries, threatened to dissolve into a mere confederation of families, each of which ensured for itself, in collaboration with clergymen or even with monks who lived at some distance from the city, the true—that is, the Christian—grooming of the young male.

Reading the sermons of John Chrysostom, we receive an impression of the doors of the Christian household slowly closing in on the young believer. His adolescence no longer belongs to the city. A classical culture, the privileged tool of interchange between upper-class peers, might continue to be instilled in him by schools at the traditional center of the city. But it was already a "dead" culture, derived from ancient texts, still held to be necessary for correct writing and speaking, but whose connection with daily life had been severed. The young Christian's code of deportment no longer derived from the same source that it would have two centuries earlier. The deportment of the Christian believer is now revealed most clearly in the lifestyle of the monk. This amounted to an education in the fear of God, which could be observed in contemporary monastic circles to cut far deeper into the personality than did the old-fashioned civic fear of incurring shame in the presence of the wellborn. It was mediated in an environment that was more intimate and more stable than that provided by the upper-class youth group. Chrysostom saved the young Antiochene boy from the city, in order to hand him over to the subtle dread of his own father. Chrysostom, a great psychologist of religious awe, now saw the fear of God, instilled every day in the growing boy by the weighty

Painted glass, 5th century(?). Two women in court costume with a young prince, all Christians; we do not know who they are. (Christian Museum of Brescia.)

presence of the Christian father, as the basis of a new, and Christian, code of deportment.

At a stroke, we glimpse early Byzantine Antioch as it could yet be. No longer a Hellenistic city, the behavior of its leading citizens is no longer subtly molded by codes derived from life in ancient public centers. The ancient public spaces are ignored. Theater and forum are absent. Winding, narrow lanes lead back and forth from great religious gatherings in the Christian basilica, to secluded courtyards in whose screened privacy the believing father passes on to his sons the religious art of the fear of God. It is a glimpse into the future, to the Islamic town.

Yet the glimpse is misleading. Passing from the sermons of John Chrysostom to the epitaphs of his contemporaries, in Greek and Latin, we catch a very different sight of the urban Christian. He had remained to the end a man of public space. If no longer a "lover of his town," he was instead a "lover of the people of God," or a "lover of the poor." Apart from a few gravestones of monks and clergymen, hardly a single inscription stressed the intimate motive force of the fear of God in the Christian believer. The Christian layman had remained an ancient man, gloriously sensitive to those ancient adjectives that acclaimed his relations with his fellows. He was far less concerned to lay bare for posterity motives that we know to have caused his heroes, the monks, to sigh and shudder throughout their lives in salutary dread.

Silver wedding casket (detail), found in Rome, 379–382. Intended as a gift for a Christian bride, Prospecta, the casket is carried into the groom's home. (London, British Museum.)

Asceticism and Marriage

Of all the aspects of the life of the settled community upon which the monastic paradigm laid a vast, impalpable burden, the most intimate was that associated with marriage, with intercourse within marriage, and with the role of sexuality. The Christian household might be expected to close its doors to the forum and the theater as places for the grooming of the young; but it was called upon to open the doors of the bedchamber to a new awareness of the nature of sexuality, developed among the continent "men of the desert." The varying degrees to which such households opened that door— or, to be more precise, were expected to do so by their bishops, clergy, and spiritual advisers—takes us to the beginning of the contrast between the Christian societies of Byzantium and of the Catholic West throughout the Middle Ages.

Sarcophagus of Junius Bassus, ca. 359. In this consecrated rural setting and a dignified atmosphere, Adam and Eve feel shame for the sin they have committed. (Rome, Vatican Grottoes.)

 East and West: The New Marital Morality

T HE monastic paradigm had placed a question mark after marriage, sexuality, and even the differentiation of the sexes. In Paradise, Adam and Eve had been asexual beings. Their decline from an "angelic" state of single-hearted worship of God was assisted, if not directly caused, by a decline into sexuality. This decline into sexuality started the fatal slide of men and women into a world of double-hearted cares associated with marriage, with childbirth, and with hard labor to support hungry mouths.

The story of the Fall of mankind, in the persons of Adam and Eve, was held to be a faithful mirror of the soul of the contemporary ascetic, trembling on the brink of commitment to the dire restraints of life "in the world," and summoning up the resolution to opt for the "angelic" life of the monk. For in the cramped world of the Near Eastern villages, as among the dour households of the urban Christians, entry into the world began, in practice, with a parentally arranged marriage for the young couple in their early teens.

Told in this radical form, as pointing the road to a Paradise Regained in the desert, monasticism threatened to wash away some of the firmest supports of settled life in the eastern Mediterranean. It implied that married Christians could not hope to enter Paradise, which was accessible only to those who in this life had adopted the sexual abstinence of Adam and Eve before their fall into sexuality and into marriage. If the life of the monk was thought to foreshadow the paradisiacal state of an asexual human nature, then man and woman—as monk and virgin, their sexuality eliminated by being renounced—might yet wander together over the bleak mountainsides of Syria, as Adam and Eve had once stood, upon the flowering slopes of Paradise, untouched by gender and by its present, disturbing sexual ache.

One of six surviving diptychs of Anastasius. Consul in Byzantium in 517, he holds the handkerchief that he will throw down to signal the start of a race. He also staged animal hunts. Here one of the hunters is bitten by a hyena, and others attempt to lasso lions. (Paris, Bibliothèque Nationale, Cabinet des Médailles.)

The threat of an obliteration of gender, with a resulting indifference to sexuality as an element to be feared in the relations of men and women, was the *Grande Peur* (Great Fear) of the fourth-century Eastern world. It provoked immediate reactions from monks and clergy alike. A shrill misogyny is the modern reader's first impression of much monastic literature. The citation *All flesh is grass* was interpreted as meaning that men and women, as indelibly sexual beings, were permanently liable to instantaneous combustion! The good monk was supposed to carry even his own mother across a stream, carefully shrouded in his cloak, "for the touch of the flesh of a woman is as fire." Behind such bruising anecdotes lies the incessant challenge of a radical alternative. In radical Christian ascetic groups, denial of the value of marriage tended to go hand in hand with a denial of sexuality itself. This, in turn, implied a denial of the division between the world and the desert. For those whose feet already trod the slopes of Paradise in this life, by opting for the "angelic" existence of the monk or the virgin, might pass with eyes as innocent as those of a child through the countryside, through the villages, and through the crowded towns, mingling unrestrained with men and women alike. Athanasius had to challenge the followers of Hierakas on this issue in Egypt. Hierakas, a revered ascetic thinker, had doubted whether married persons had any place in Paradise and, at the same time, expected his austere followers to be ministered to with impunity by virgin female companions. Chrysostom preached against "spiritual partnerships" of monks and virgins within the city of Antioch. Later the stirrings of the Messalian monks, monks devoted to wandering and perpetual prayer and notoriously indifferent to the presence of women in their shabby ranks, became endemic in Syria and in eastern Asia Minor.

As a result of the need to contain the radicalism implicit in the monastic paradigm, the eastern Mediterranean became a society explicitly organized, in a shriller manner than ever before, in terms of a democracy of sexual shame. All persons, from the married heads of upper-class families to the heroic men of the desert, were expected to share a common code of sexual avoidance, irrespective of class and profession. In Antioch, Chrysostom even dared attack the public baths, social gathering point par excellence of civic upper-class society. He criticized aristocratic ladies for exposing themselves before the eyes of troops of servants, their softly nurtured flesh draped only in the heavy jewelry that was the mark of high status.

In Alexandria even the scanty dress of the poor was thought to create distressing fantasies in the believer, in a manner inconceivable in previous centuries where such exposure might be treated as contemptible but was hardly feared as a source of automatic moral danger.

As for members of married Christian households in the eastern Mediterranean, in this and in later periods, we are faced with a paradox. The heroes and spiritual advisers of the *kosmikoi,* "the men in the world," tended to be "men of the desert." The kosmikoi dearly loved to walk out to visit them or to receive them into their houses, their very bodies exuding the "sweet smell of the desert." As we have just seen, the monastic literature produced by the men of the desert generated an exceptional amount of overt anxiety on the issue of sexual avoidance. It presented the sexual drive as potentially operative, for the bad, in all social situations between men and women. Yet, beyond that, the concern of the men of the desert with sexuality followed lines that were strictly parallel to those of the married men in the world.

The spiritual masters of the desert, most notably Evagrius and his Latin exponent, John Cassian, came to treat the fact

Syrian relief, ca. 200. The Syrian woman is invisible beneath her veils; the Syrian goddess has become a nude Venus. Below, Astarté-Venus, goddess of nature, and her lover, Adonis, oriental god of rebirth, here stylized as a Greek hero. At the left is a model of a round temple offered by the couple; above and below can be seen a schematic representation of folds in the temple curtain. (Paris, Louvre.)

of sexuality as a privileged sensor of the spiritual condition of the monk. Sexually based imaginations, the manifestation of sexual drives in dreams and through night emissions, were examined with a sensitivity unheard of in previous traditions of introspection, and in a manner entirely independent of any opportunities for contact with the other sex. To see sexuality in this manner was a revolutionary change of viewpoint. From being regarded as a source of "passions," whose anomalous promptings might disrupt the harmony of the well-groomed person if triggered by objects of sexual desire, sexuality came to be treated as a symptom that betrayed other passions. It became the privileged window through which the monk could peer into the most private reaches of his soul. In the tradition of Evagrius, sexual imaginings were scrutinized minutely in and of themselves. They were held to reveal concretely (if shamefully) the presence in the soul of yet more deadly, because more faceless drives: the cold cramp of anger, pride, and avarice. Hence the abatement of sexual imaginings, even the modification of night emissions, was closely observed as an index for the monk of the extent to which he had won through to a state of single-hearted translucence to the love of God and of his neighbors. "For you have possessed my innermost parts," wrote Cassian, reporting the discourse of Apa Chaeremon. "And so he shall be found in the night as he is in the day, in bed as when at prayer, alone as when he is surrounded by crowds."[12] The slow remittance of the lingering, intensely private meanings associated with sexual dreams heralded the passing away from the soul of those far greater beasts, anger and pride, distant echoes of whose heavy tread appeared in the form of sexual fantasies. With this the monk had closed the last, razor-thin fissure in the single heart.

The doctrine of sexuality as a privileged symptom of personal transformation was the most consequential rendering ever achieved of the ancient Jewish and Christian yearning for the single heart. In the hands of an intellectual such as Evagrius, it was the most original approach to introspection to come from the late antique world. Yet it scarcely touched on the experience of the laity. The doors of the Christian household, which we have sensed closing silently between the young Christian and the claims of his city as the source of moral guidance, closed also against the strange new sense of sexuality developed, among themselves and for themselves, by the men of the desert. The marital and sexual morality of the early Byzantine Christian was dour; but little in it seemed

Ivory plate. A bearded Christ is flanked by Peter and Paul and scenes from New Testament. (Paris, Bibliothèque Nationale, Cabinet des Médailles.)

problematic. Its rules provided a clear guide for those young persons who wished to remain in the world. Throughout the Byzantine Near East the norms of married life were as familiar, and as seemingly unshakable in their own way, as were the structures of secular law and administration that still ringed the Near East in the age of Justinian with the sense of an Empire, with frontiers "firm as statues of bronze."

In Eastern Christian morality the facts of sexuality were not communicated by the clergy as fraught with any particular sense of mystery. Either one lived with them, as a married person, in the world, or one abandoned them, in order to soak the body in the "sweet smell of the desert." The latter choice was best made at an early age; the age of stormy, middle-aged conversions to the ascetic life had passed. By A.D. 500 it was important that the young man, and especially that the very young girl, should make up their minds for or against continuing to live as a married person in the world, before the heavy social restraints of betrothal came to weigh in on them in their early teens. Uncertainty after that point could lead only to the disruptive consequences of an unsatisfied yearning for the desert in later, married life. Very often the choice that one of the parents might have made was postponed

Convent of Saint Simeon (Qal'at Saman), ca. 470. Thirty-odd miles northwest of Aleppo, this was a masterpiece in a severe style, monumental yet airy, in which the language of ancient architecture was still alive.

for a generation, by being passed on to one of the children. The sixth century is a century of child saints, of infant recruits to the ascetic life. Martha, the pious mother of Simeon the Younger of Antioch, raised her son to become a famous stylite, or pillar-squatting, saint (at the age of seven!) because she herself had been married off against her will to a newly arrived artisan–colleague of her father. Young Simeon was a substitute for Martha's own yearning for sanctity, cut short, as was so often the case, by an arranged marriage.

Women in the eastern Mediterranean were shunned more carefully than before. Ancient imaginative boundaries between the sexes were reemphasized, including the exclusion of menstruating women from the Eucharist. Yet in Byzantine cities most people lived in close quarters, usually off a single central courtyard; sexual segregation must have been largely notional. The architecture of the harem, of a totally separate living quarter for women, had not yet appeared in the Christian cities of the sixth-century Near East. Among the males it was known that the "heats" of youth could be discharged through premarital sex. The only contribution of the ascetic tradition on this point was a tendency to ask even male penitents if they had "lost their virginity," and under what circumstances. It

Reliefs on wooden doors, ca. 432. One of the most ancient images of the crucifixion. Christ's cross, almost never depicted in early Christian art, does not appear. The noble architecture in the background, historically ridiculous, makes the scene unrealistic and represents, inaccurately, the church with three entries built by Constantine at Calvary. (Rome, Church of Santa Sabina.)

would have been a very strange question indeed to ask three hundred years earlier of a man for whom "virginity" was the exclusive concern of his sisters and daughters.

Byzantine Realities

Early marriage was proposed for the young of both sexes as a breakwater that could shield Christian men from the choppy seas of adolescent promiscuity. Yet even such a moralist as Chrysostom could see little problematic in the act of sex within the stilled waters of lawful wedlock. Ancient restrictions still hedged in the act of intercourse, but they were largely concerned with when or how it should be performed. The time-honored imposition of withdrawal from the woman in times of menstruation and during pregnancy had been compounded by the obligation to abstain during church fasts and festivals. When permitted, however, the intercourse between married partners was taken for granted. What is more, medical opinion continued to assert that only through a passionate and pleasurable discharge, experienced by both the man and the woman in a hot act of love, could the conception of the child be guaranteed and, with it, the quality of its "temperament"—that balance of hot and cold humors that might make it a boy or a girl, a healthy or a morbid character.

Let us look back at the world of the early Byzantine men in the world, flanked now, if at a safe distance, by the imposing men of the desert. We see the outlines of a very ancient urban society in its final days.

Beyond the doors of the basilica and the gates of the Christian household, the city had remained stridently profane and sexually undisciplined. In the city, although it might now be supported by Christian notables in the name of an ostentatiously pious Christian emperor, nude girls of the lower classes continued to delight the upper-class citizens of Constantinople; they splashed in great aquatic spectacles in Antioch, Gerasa, and elsewhere. In the "Blessed City" of Edessa, oldest Christian city in the Near East, pantomime dancers still whirled sinuously in the theater. A nude statue of Venus stood outside the public baths of Alexandria—allegedly causing the robes of adulterous ladies to blow up over their heads—until it was finally removed, not by a bishop but by the local Muslim governor, at the end of the seventh century. As late as 630 in Palermo three hundred prostitutes rioted against the Byzantine governor as he entered the public baths. (We know of the incident only because the governor, a good Byzantine

Detail of sarcophagus, 4th century. Adam and Eve after the Fall, facing eviction from Eden. (Velletri, Communal Museum.)

who expected the clergy to do their duty by their city, had met clerical demands by appointing the bishop Imperial Inspector of Brothels—thereby earning the rebuke of a shocked Western pope!) What remained of the ancient city in the Byzantine East had evidently not rallied in all its aspects to the moral codes exemplified for the laity by the monks.

Laity and Clergy in the West

In looking at the problems posed by sexuality, not from the "desert" and the "world" of Byzantium but through the eyes of Augustine, the Catholic bishop of Hippo, and of subsequent Latin clergymen, we can sense the outlines of another, different world that would form around the bishops of the Catholic Church in the provinces of the post-Imperial West.

The monastic paradigm, based on a sense of the presocial

and presexual glory of Adam and Eve, did not haunt the urban bishop of the Latin West as it so plainly tantalized and disturbed the bishops of the eastern Mediterranean. With Augustine, its basic assumption was firmly abandoned. Human society, including marriage and sexuality, was by no means a second best, interim stage of humanity, rendered impalpable by nostalgia for a lost "angelic" majesty of man. For Augustine, Adam and Eve had never been asexual beings. They would have enjoyed in Paradise a full marital existence; the joys of continuity through children would have been granted to them. Augustine saw no reason whatsoever why such children should not have been begotten and conceived by an act of intercourse accompanied by sensations of solemn and sharp delight. Paradise, for the bishop of Hippo, was no shimmering antithesis to life "in the world," but a "place of peace and harmonious joys"—that is, not the absence of settled society, as the desert was, but settled society as it should be, shorn of the tensions inherent in its present condition. Paradise and the experience of Adam and Eve there provided a paradigm of social, even sexual, interchange, against which to judge—and, given the fallen condition of man, find wanting—the most intimate sexual deportment of the married laity. For if Paradise could be presented as a fully social state, a shadow of Paradise Regained could be seen not only, as in Byzantium, in the vast silences of a desert, at a distance from organized human life, but even in the solemn hierarchy of service and command, within the basilicas of the Catholic church in the cities. Part of this Paradise Regained would be associated not just with the clear-cut, public abandonment of marriage for the desert, but with the intensely private endeavor of married couples to equate their own sexual behavior to the harmonious innocence first exemplified, in married sexuality, by Adam and Eve.

In such a view sexuality ceased to be an anomaly whose importance faded into relative insignificance when compared with the far greater anomaly of man's sad decline from the angelic state. Unlike Evagrius and John Cassian, therefore, Augustine could not hope to see sexuality fade away from the imagination of a single-hearted few, schooled in the vast solitudes of the desert. Nor could he follow the Byzantine householder and his spiritual guides in treating sexuality within marriage as of little interest, provided that it was entered into within traditional forms of social restraint. As long as sexuality was dwarfed by a sense of the vast sadness of mortality, it posed few problems. It was possible for John Chrysostom and other Greek bishops to present intercourse as no more than an untidy, but necessary, means of securing continuity through the begetting of children. Chrysostom indeed could acclaim it as a positive boon, which had been granted by God to Adam after his Fall, so that human beings, fallen from their angelic majesty into death, could seek a fleeting shadow of eternity through begetting children. For Augustine, by contrast, sexuality was as intimate a symptom of the Fall of Adam and Eve as was mortality; its present, uncontrollable nature resulted from the Fall as immediately and as surely as did the chill touch of mortality.

The anomaly of sexuality lay in its concrete experiences, which registered with sad precision the gulf between sexuality as it might have been enjoyed by Adam and Eve, had they not fallen, and the sexuality of the present, fallen Christian married couple. With the flair of an old rhetor presenting his findings as a statement of the obvious, known to all men of feeling and intelligence, pagan and Christian alike, Augustine elucidated those aspects of intercourse that seemed to betray a deep-seated dislocation of will and instinct. Erection and

Concupiscence

Silver plate, 6th century A.D. Diameter: 12 inches. Venus and Adonis. This Venus, whose small bust emphasizes her full hips, reflects a taste for realism that classical canons had consigned to the minor arts. The male nude is well built. The pillar is a clumsy means of breaking the symmetry. The draftsmanship lacks precision, but the boldness is impressive. These are not idealized creations but two magnificent specimens of humanity. Byzantine work. (Paris, Bibliothèque Nationale, Cabinet des Médailles.)

Syrian plaque, 6th century.
One of the two Saints Simeon,
seated atop the column, around
which a serpent has wrapped
itself. The ladder symbolizes
the difficulty faced by the soul
in ascending to heaven. Images
of the two stylites were among
the first to attract cults.

orgasm hold his attention, for the will seemed to have no access to either, in that neither could the impotent (or frigid) summon up such a sensation by an act of will nor, once summoned, could such sensations be controlled by the will. For Augustine these were vivid and apparently irreversible tokens in all human beings, men and women, married and continent, of the wrath of God against the pride of Adam and Eve in cutting themselves off from the will of God. An ageless, faceless, and protean "concupiscence of the flesh" capable of manifesting itself in such very precise symptoms in the intercourse of married persons and requiring constant moral vigilance also among the continent, was the sign of a fateful dislocation of the former harmony of man and God, of body and soul, of male and female, enjoyed by Adam and Eve. They had lived in Paradise not as asexual celibates but as a fully married human couple, and so as much an embryonic human society as any Christian householder of Hippo. The juxtaposition of an ideal human married state with the actual married life of the lay person was a comparison as potent and as pointed as it was invidious to the average couple.

Such views, or variants of such views, have become so much a part of the bloodstream of Western Christendom, that it is important to step back a little in order to sense their first strangeness and to appreciate the particularity of the situation that led Augustine and his successors to modify, in so significant a manner, the monastic paradigm that they had inherited from the East.

For the Christian layman nothing less was at stake than a new interpretation of the meaning of sex. The new interpretation implied the obsolescence of the codes of deportment rooted on a specific physiological model of the human person. Both the codes and the physiology had conspired in the Antonine age to harness the energies of sexual passion to a specific model of society. The doctors and moralists of the period had attempted to absorb sexuality into the good order of the city. They had taken for granted that a vigorous discharge of "generative heat," mobilized throughout the body as a whole in both man and woman and accompanied by clear sensations of physical pleasure, was a sine qua non of conception. Conception and passion could not be disjoined. The only problem for the moralist was that such passion should not sap the public deportment of the male by being indulged in frivolously or excessively in private. Furthermore, it was widely believed that intercourse that took place according to norms of decorum that were in some manner continuous with public codes of deportment would produce better children than would intercourse in which such norms had been flouted, whether by oral foreplay, by inappropriate postures, or by access to the woman in menstruation. In such a way, the sexual act might be presented as the most intimate token of the "morality of social distance" associated with the maintenance of the codes of public decorum specific to the upper classes.

Augustine dismantled this model; his views implied nothing less than a new body image. Sexual passion was no longer presented primarily as a diffused and mindless bodily "heat" brought to a peak in intercourse. Attention was focused instead on precise zones of specifically sexual feeling: for men, the nature of the erection and the precise quality of the ejaculation. These were weaknesses in which all human beings shared equally. As a result, the more brutal forms of misogyny were muted, in Augustine's thought at least, if not in day-to-day practice in the early medieval West. It was less credible to claim that women had more sexuality than men, or that they sapped men's reason by provoking them to sensuality. Men were as passive to deep-seated sexual frailty, in Augustine's opinion, as were women. Both bore in their unruly bodies the same fatal symptom of the Fall of Adam and Eve. The fact of the swamping of the conscious mind in orgasm for both parties eclipsed the ancient Roman dread of "effeminacy," of a weakening of the public person through passionate dependence on inferiors of either sex.

The surprisingly tenacious belief that upper-class decorum in bed might contribute to the begetting of "well-conceived" children—healthy, biddable, preferably male—was superseded by a new sense of the sexual act as a moment of inevitable disjunction from the rational, which meant in effect from the social, aspects of the person. The "concupiscence of the flesh," as revealed in the sexual act, was a streak of the human person that defied social definition and could only be touched externally by social restraint. For the layman and laywoman normal restraints on intercourse, which had been largely of an external, social nature, had to include a new sense of a fissure deep within the texture of the act. Ultimately God created and formed the child; the sexual act by which the partners provided the material for His creative act owed nothing whatsoever, even in the most remote manner, to the subtle and penetrating disciplines of the city.

Whether such bleak and novel thoughts cast a chill over

the sexual relations of late Roman couples in the West is an entirely different matter. One suspects that they did not. This in itself is silent testimony to the strength of the ancient ways of life, in the face of Christian clerical leadership. Christian couples continued to believe their doctors: in any case, only a hot and pleasurable act of love could give them the children that justified the act of sex in the eyes of the celibate clergy. Christians were careful to avoid intercourse on forbidden days, as laid down by the church: mainly on Sundays, in Lent, and on the vigils of great feasts. They feared the genetic effects of such lapses from the new code of public decorum. Yet Augustine's emphasis on the venial sin inherent in married intercourse, though stated by him without a hint of prurience and with far greater moral tolerance than usual among late antique writers (who usually condemned out of hand all acts of sex that were not consciously entered into with the express purpose of begetting children "for the city"), did imply a sense of inappropriateness in the sensuality of married love. In the very different society of the high middle ages clergymen could believe that married love might be consciously controlled so as to minimize these inappropriate aspects, by deliberately modifying subjective enjoyment in intercourse, through controlling, for instance, forms of caress and endearment. The Augustinian doctrine had opened a crack in the door of the Christian household, such as no Byzantine had ever dreamed of opening: and through that crack many a cold wind would blow, from the canonists and their readers, the father-confessors of the later Middle Ages.

Clergy, Laity, and the Catholic Church

Augustine's views imposed an ascetic's rigor and an ascetic's awareness of human frailty on the humble householders in the world. He joined world and desert in the Catholic Church. In this he would be followed, in the silent rise of the Catholic Church in western Europe. The urban Catholic bishops of Gaul, Italy, and Spain, rather than the "men of the desert," became the arbiters of the monastic paradigm as it had been subtly and irreversibly modified by Augustine to embrace even sexuality in the world. In this form, the desert enters the city, and it does so from above. Desert and world no longer operate parallel to each other, as remained the case in Byzantium. Instead we have a new hierarchy, in which a continent clergy, frequently trained, as were Augustine's clergy, in urban monastic communities, came to govern the laity, largely by means of disciplining and advising them on the perpetual, shared anomaly of a fallen sexuality.

Apart from this one, clear hierarchy, we see a social structure flattened beneath the gaze of the old bishop of Hippo. Men and women, the wellborn and their inferiors, the "men of the desert" as inescapably, if less luridly, as the married "men in the world," were all held to share in a universal and aboriginal weakness in the form of a sexual nature inherited in its dislocated form from Adam and Eve. No renunciation could raise a person above it; no studiously internalized code could do anything more than contain it. This dislocation was presented as a privileged, because a singularly intimate and apposite, symptom of the human condition. Man as a sexual being had become the lowest common denominator in the great democracy of sinners gathered into the Catholic Church.

Around 1200 a minor writer of confessional manuals declared: "Of all the battles of the Christians, the struggle for chastity is the most great. There, combat is constant and victory is rare. Continence, indeed, is the Great War. For, as Ovid says . . . and as Juvenal reminds us . . . Claudian also . . . As do Saint Jerome and Saint Augustine."[13]

In all later writings of the Latin church, it is notable how the vivid love poetry of ancient Rome and the somber warnings of the Christian writers of the late antique period blur together. They communicate a strange sense that it is sexuality and not, as for Byzantines, haunted still by the mirage of a Paradise Regained in the deep desert, the darker and more faceless pride and violence of the world that has become the privileged concern, the horror, and even the delight, of the western European.

Tombstone, 5th century. Baptism was most commonly administered when a person reached adulthood. Water was poured over him, in this case by a dove representing the Holy Spirit. As usual, the baptized person is shown smaller than the other figures. (Aquileia, Christian Museum of Monastero.)

Notes

Bibliography

Acknowledgments

Index

Notes

1. Musonius Rufus, fragment 14, ed. and trans. Cora E. Lutz, *Yale Classical Studies,* 10 (1947): 93. The words quoted in the next paragraph are from fragment 12, p. 87.

2. II *Baruch* 85.3; lines in the next paragraph are from II *Baruch* 85.4.

3. Cited in E. Urbach, *The Sages: Their Concepts and Beliefs* (Jerusalem: Magnus, 1979), p. 358.

4. Galen, cited in an Arabic author; see R. Walzer, *Galen on Jews and Christians* (Oxford: Oxford University Press, 1949), p. 15.

5. F. Nietzsche, *Die fröhliche Wissenschaft* 358 (Stuttgart: Kroner Taschenbuch, 1956): 251.

6. *Sentences of Sextus* no. 236.

7. J. Doresse and E. Lanne, *Un témoin archaïque de la liturgie copte de S. Gasile* (Louvain: Bibliothèque de Muséon, 1960), p. 28.

8. John Chrysostom, *Homily 11 in 2 Thessalonians* and *Homily 1 in Titus,* trans. Library of the Nicene Fathers (Grand Rapids, Mich.: Eerdmans, 1979), 13:373, 479.

9. E. Diehl, *Inscriptiones latinae christianae veteres,* no. 2157 (Berlin: Wiedman, 1925), 1:423. The following paragraph closes with *Inscriptiones* no. 967, p. 179.

10. *Historia Monachorum* 10.

11. John Chrysostom, *On Virginity* 73.1.

12. John Cassian, *Collationes* 12.8.

13. Cited in M. Mueller, *Die Lehre von dem heilige Augustinus von der Paradiesehe* (Regensburg: F. Pustet, 1954), p. 152, n. 79.

Bibliography

Although recent historiography of the later Empire has produced many reliable surveys of the political, social, and religious history of the late antique period, it offers no single treatment of the age from the viewpoint of this series. The short work of a master is closest to such a survey: H.-I. Marrou, *Décadence romaine ou antiquité tardive?* (Paris, 1977). In the English-speaking world, William Lecky, *History of European Morals from Augustus to Charlemagne* (London, 1869), summarizes a traditional attitude. A. H. M. Jones, *The Latter Roman Empire*, vol. II (Oxford, 1964), esp. pp. 873–1024, contains much evidence but little comment. Without the work of Paul Veyne, I would have lacked not only the information necessary to venture along this new path but also the courage, which I owe largely to his vigor and deep erudition in handling subjects rarely approached in the same manner by other scholars.

The world of the city: P. Veyne, *Le Pain et le Cirque* (Paris: Seuil, 1976), and R. MacMullen, *Paganism in the Roman Empire* (New Haven: Yale University Press, 1981). Education and socialization in the city: H.-I. Marrou, *Histoire de l'éducation dans l'Antiquité* (Paris, 1948; reprint, Paris: Seuil, 1981, 2 vols.), remains unsurpassed; this is true also of A. J. Festugière, *Antioche païenne et chrétienne* (Paris, 1959), esp. pp. 211–240. A. C. Dionisotti, "From Ausonius' Schooldays? A Schoolbook and Its Relatives," *Journal of Roman Studies,* 82 (1982): 83, makes available a charming new document.

Sexuality, deportment, and medical images of the body: P. Veyne, "La famille et l'amour sous le Haut Empire romain," *Annales,* 33 (1978): 35, and "L'homosexualité à Rome," *Communications,* 35 (1982): 26, represent a new starting point for discussion; Aline Rousselle, *Porneia: de la maîtrise du corps à la privation sensorielle* (Paris, 1983), is exceptionally illuminating. The stability of normative values on inscriptions: L. Robert, *Hellenica,* 13 (1965): 226–227, to begin with, as any other of the many passages dedicated to such issues form the pen of an unrivaled connoisseur of the Greek world under the Empire.

Social distance: R. MacMullen, *Roman Social Relations* (New Haven: Yale University Press, 1974), is convincing. *Popularitas* and the moral quality of the shows: L. Robert, *Les gladiateurs dans l'Orient grec* (Paris, 1940), sees an ugly matter with unfailing precision; see also G. Ville and P. Veyne, "Religion et politique: comment ont pris fin les combats de gladiateurs," *Annales,* 34 (1979): 651. The democratization of philosophical ideals in Christian circles: H. E. Chadwick, *The Sentences of Sixtus* (Cambridge, Eng., 1959), and the humane and learned introduction and notes of H.-I. Marrou (with M. Harl) to *Clément d'Alexandrie: Le Pédagogue,* Sources chrétiennes 70 (Paris, 1960).

On the "heart" and the "evil inclination" in late Judaism, J. Hadot, *Penchant mauvais et volonté libre dans la Sagesse de Ben Sira* (Brussels, 1972), is a good introduction; G. F. Moore, *Judaism* (Cambridge, Mass.: Harvard University Press, 1950), pp. 474–496, assembles the rabbinic evidence. The sociology of the early Christian community in Corinth has been studied by G. Theissen, especially in articles in *Zeitschrift für neutestamentliche Wissenschaft,* 65 (1974): 232, *Novum Testamentum,* 16 (1974): 179, and *Evangelische Theologie,* 35 (1975): 155: these are translated in *The Social Setting of Pauline Christianity* (Philadelphia, 1982). Wayne Meeks, the *First Urban Christians: The Social World of the Apostle Paul* (New Haven: Yale University Press, 1983), represents a quantum-jump in sociological sophistication. For the remaining centuries, we are left with the work of an *Altmeister,* A. Harnack, *Mission und Ausbreitung des Christentums* (Leipzig, 1902). H. Gülzow, Kallist von Rom, *Zeitschrift für neutestamentliche Wissenschaft,* 58 (1968): 102, and L. W. Countryman, *The Rich Christian in the Church of the Early Empire* (New York, 1980), are revealing.

On alsmgiving and shifts in popular morality, P. Veyne, *Le pain et le cirque,* pp. 44–50, and remarks in "Suicide, Fisc, esclavage capital et droit romain," *Latomus,* 40 (1981): 217, are the best starting point. Celibacy and marital rigorism in the Early Church: C. Munier, *L'Église dans l'empire romain* (Paris, 1979), pp. 7–16, is a clear summary. *Etica sessuale e matrimonio nel cristianes-imo delle origini,* ed. R. Cantalamassa (Milan, 1976) contains some excellent essays, esp. P. F. Beatrice, "Continenza e matrimonio nel cristianesimo primitivo," p. 3; *Les Actes Apocryphes des Apôtres: Christianisme et monde païen,* ed. F. Bovon (Geneva, 1981), touches on related issues. On the issue of sexual renunciation in late antiquity, I am in disagreement with the luminous little book of E. R. Dodds, *Pagan, and Christian in an Age of Anxiety* (Cambridge, Eng., 1965).

Social structure and city life in the later Empire: Peter Brown, *The Making of Late Antiquity* (Cambridge, Mass.: Harvard University Press, 1978), pp. 27–53, advances an interpretation and assembles much secondary literature; C. Lepelley, *Les cités de l'Afrique romaine au Bas-Empire,* 2 vols. (Paris, 1979–1981), is a definitive addition; see also R. Krautheimer, *Three Christian Capitals: Topography and Politics* (Berkeley, 1983). On costume: R. MacMullen, "Some Pictures in Ammianus Marcellinus," *Art Bulletin* (1964): 49, and G. Fabre, "Recherches sur l'origine des ornements vestimentaires du Bas-Empire," *Karthago,* 16 (1973): 107; acute and concrete, Marrou, *Décadence romaine,* pp. 15–20, sees the importance of such changes.

Urban ceremonial and the mystique of power: H. Stern, *Le Calendrier de 354* (Paris, 1953), remains essential; M. Meslin, *La fête des kalendes de janvier* (Brussels, 1970), describes a significant mutation in pagan folklore; J. W. Salomonson, *Voluptatem spectandi non perdat sed mutet* (Amsterdam, 1979), illustrates the continuity of a mystique of the games in Christian circles. The relation between the palaces of the *potentes* and the ideology of their power registered in mosaics has been recently studied by K. M. D. Dunbabin, *The Mosaics of Roman North Africa* (Oxford, 1978). The mosaics of the villa at Piazza Armerina in Sicily have provoked much discussion; see S. Settis, "Per l'inter-pretazione di Piazza Armerina," *Mélanges d'archéologie et d'histoire: Antiquité,* 87 (1975): 873; for the discovery of similar mosaics at Tellaro and Patti, see Lellia Cracco Ruggini, *La Sicilia tra Roma e Bisanzio: Storia di Sicilia* (Naples, 1982), III, 66.

City and basilica: R. Krautheimer, *Rome: Profile of a City* (Princeton, 1980), is a masterly supplement to the monumental study of C. Pietri, *Roma cristiana,* 2 vols. (Paris, 1977). For changes in ecclesiastical ceremonial and almsgiving, see Peter Brown, "Dalla plebs romana alla plebs Dei. Aspetti della cristianizzazione di Roma," *Passatopresente,* 2 (1982): 123, and *The Cult of the Saints: Its Rise and Function in Latin Christianity* (Chicago, 1981), pp. 39–49. On poverty and almsgiving, E. Patlagean, *Pauvreté économique et pauvreté sociale à Byzance* (Paris, 1977), marks a new departure in the study of late Roman society and the influence of Christianity on the urban community.

The idiosyncracy of pagan epitaphs is well presented by R. Lattimore, *Themes in Greek and Latin Epitaphs* (Urbana, Ill., 1962). the care of the dead in Christian communities receives outstanding treatment by P. A. Février, "Le Culte des morts dans les communautés chrétiennes durant le iiième siecle," *Atti del ix° congresso di archeologia cristiana* (Rome, 1977), I, 212, and "À propos du culte funéraire: culte et sociabilité," *Cahiers archéologiques,* 26 (1977): 29, and by R. Krautheimer, "Mensa, coemeterium, martyrium," *Cahiers archéologiques,* 11 (1960): 15. These and others contributed to the interpretation in Brown, *Cult of the Saints,* pp. 23–38. B. Young, "paganisme, christianisme et rites funéraires mérovingiens," *Archéologie mediévale,* 7 (1977): 5, is an important contribution for one region; Y. Duval, *Loca sanctorum Africae* (Rome: École française de Rome, 1982), is a magnificent collection for another. V. Saxer, *Morts, martyrs, reliques en Afrique chrétienne* (Paris, 1980), documents clerical attitudes.

For the antecedents of monastic spirituality, see A. Guillaumont, "Monachisme et éthique judéo-chrétienne," *Judéo-Christianisme: volume offert au cardinal J. Daniélou: Recherches de science religieuse,* 60 (1972): 199. The impact of monasticism is best approached through the work of its major exponents in an urban environment: *Jean Chrysostome: La Virginité,* ed. B. Grillet, Sources chrétiennes 125 (Paris, 1966), and *Grégoire de Nysse: Traité sur la Virginité,* ed. M. Aubineau, Sources chrétiennes 119 (Paris, 1966)—the latter particularly useful. The theoretical radicalism of the monastic paradigm can lend itself to serious exaggeration of the rigor of the ascetic practices of the monks; not even the best accounts are immune, notably Festugière, *Antioche,* pp. 291–310, and A. Vööbus, *A History of Asceticism in the Syrian Orient,* vols. 1 and 2 (Louvain, 1958 and 1960). D. Chitty, *The Desert a City* (Oxford, 1966), an exceptionally learned and humane book, and E. A. Judge, "The Earliest Use of 'Monachos,'" *Jahrbuch für Antike und Christentum,* 20 (1977): 72, provide correctives. Monastic poverty and its relation to the self-image of a Christian society, shown to be crucial by Patlagean, *Pauvreté,* has been studied in the Pachomian communities by B. Büchler, *Die Armut der Armen* (Munich, 1980). Oxyrhynchus is discussed in J. M. Carrié, "Les distributions alimentaires dans les cités de l'empire romain tardif," *Mélanges d'archéologie et d'histoire: Antiquité,* 87 (1975): 995, and by R. Remondon, "L'église dans la societé égyptienne à l'époque byzantine," *Chronique d'Égypte,* 47

(1972): 254. Monastic education and the city: Festugière, *Antioche,* pp. 181–240, and Marrou, *Histoire de l'éducation,* pp. 149–161, see issues clearly; *Jean Chrysostome: Sur la vaine gloire,* ed. A. M. Malingrey, Sources chrétiennes 188 (Paris, 1972), is the most revealing source. On monastic introspection and sexuality: F. Refoulé, "Rêves et vie spirituelle d'apres Évagre le Pontique," *La vie spirituelle: Supplément,* 14 (1961): 470; M. Foucault, "Le combat de la chasteté," *Communications,* 35 (1982): 15, and A. Rouselle, *Porneia,* pp. 167–250, are new approaches to a topic usually covered with platitudes in scholarly treatments; *Évagre le Pontique: Traité pratique ou le moine,* 2 vols., ed. A. and C. Guillaumont, Sources chrétiennes 170 and 171 (Paris, 1971), is invaluable.

Byzantine marital morality and urban conditions: C. Scaglioni, "Ideale coniugale e familiare in san Giovanni Crisostomo," *Etica sessuale,* ed. Cantalamessa, p. 273, and the contributions in *Jean Chrysostome et Augustin,* ed. C. Kannengiesser (Paris, 1975), mark a beginning. *Barsanuphe et Jean de Gaza: Correspondence,* trans. L. Regnault (Solesmes, 1971), gives a delightful picture of the moral problems on which laymen and monks sought the advice of a local holy man. Sexuality as a remedy for mortality in Greek Christian thought: Ton H. C. van Eijk, "Marriage and Virginity, Death and Immortality," *Epektasis: Mélanges J. Daniélou* (Paris, 1972), p. 209, is the most important study.

A. Kazhdan and A. Cutler, "Continuity and Discontinuity in Byzantine History," *Byzantion,* 52 (1982): 429, discusses medieval Byzantine society problems that could be applied to the fifth and sixth centuries. Peter Brown, "Eastern and Western Christendom in Late Antiquity: A Parting of the Ways," *Society and the Holy in Late Antiquity* (Berkeley, 1982), p. 166, suggests the outlines of possible divergences between East and West.

The attitude of Augustine has been studied at length, but not always about the issues discussed here. Augustine's *de nuptiis et concupiscentia,* written to Count Valerius (418), is a central text, as is Book Fourteen of the *City of God* (420). The *de nuptiis* is edited with an excellent commentary by A. C. de Veer, *Premières polémiques contre Julien: Bibliothèque augustinienne* 23 (Paris, 1974). The letter (421?) of Augustine to the patriarch Atticus of Constantinople is a clear statement of his later views on the sexuality of Adam and Eve and on the nature of present-day concupiscence: J. Divjak, ed., *Corpus Scriptorum Ecclesiasticorum Latinorum* 88 (Vienna, 1981). I find M. Müller, *Die Lehre des heiligen Augustins von der Paradieseche und ihre Auswirkung in der Sexualethik des 12. und 13. Jahrhunderts* (Regensburg, 1954), the most reliable for the later reception of Augustinian doctrine by medieval canonists and authors of confessional manuals.

Acknowledgments

The sites and objects illustrated in this book (on the pages noted) are found in various locations, as follows: Bardo Museum, Tunis, 41, 45; Bibliothèque Nationale, Paris, 57; Bibliothèque Nationale, Cabinet des Médailles, Paris, 45, 47, 62, 65, 71; British Museum, London, 59; Catacombs of Saint January, 43; Cathedral, Aquileia, 53; Christian Museum of Brescia, 58; Christian Museum of the Lateran, Rome, 44, 46; Christian Museum of Monastero, Aquileia, 75; Church of Saint Ambrose, Milan, 48; Church of Santa Sabina, Rome, 67; Communal Museum, Velletri, 69; Crypt of Santa Maria, Verona, 31; Curia, Rome, 25; Episcopal Museum, Trier, 48; Landesmuseum, Trier, 2, 35, 39; Louvre, Paris, 13, 14, 20, 63; Museum of the Baths, Rome, 15, 22, 29; Museum of the Conservators, Rome, ii, 10; Museum of Fine Arts, Dijon, 19; Museum of Istanbul, 24; Museum of Saint Paul's Outside-the-Walls, Rome, 32; Palazzo, Mattei, 11; Staatsbibliothek, Berlin, 36; Vatican Grottoes, Rome, 60; Vatican Library, Rome, 3, 52; Vatican Museums, Rome, 7, 12; Vault of the Catacomb of Saint Priscilla, 16; Villa Borghese, Rome, 9.

Photographs were supplied by the following agencies and individuals: Arabesques (J.-C. et E. Chambrier), 39b, 66; Bulloz, 5, 45; G. Dagli Orti, 7, 15, 22, 24, 31, 32, 43, 53, 59; Edimédia, 41; Giraudon, 20, 62, 65; Alinari-Giraudon, 44, 58; Anderson-Giraudon, ii, 28, 42, 50; Lauros-Giraudon, 19; Magnum/E. Lessing, 16, 60, 69; C. Michaelides, 52; Roger-Viollet, 6, 13b, 55, 56; Alinari-Viollet, 12, 29; Anderson-Viollet, 46; Scala, Florence, 48b; R. Tournus, 13a, 63; private collections, 9, 25, 67.

Index